AQA Certificate in Biology (iGCSE)

Level 1/2

Niva Miles

Editor
Lawrie Ryan

REVISION GUIDE

SCIENCE

Nelson Thornes

This edition published in 2013 by:
Nelson Thornes Ltd
Delta Place
27 Bath Road
CHELTENHAM
GL53 7TH
United Kingdom

13 14 15 16 17 / 10 9 8 7 6 5 4 3

A catalogue record for this book is available from the British Library

ISBN 978 1 4085 2115 1

Cover photograph: Science Photo Library/Getty Images
Page make-up by Wearset Ltd, Boldon, Tyne and Wear

Printed and bound in Spain by GraphyCems

Photo acknowledgements
B1.5.2 Peter Arnold Inc./Alamy; B2.1.2 Science Photo Library; B3.2.2
J C Revy, ISM/Science Photo Library; B3.4.1 Alex Yeung/Fotolia; B3.4.2
Martyn Chillmaid; B4.2.1 Penny Tweedie/Science Photo Library; B4.2.2
BSIP Laurent/Trunyo/Science Photo Library; B4.5.1 Steve Cole Images/
iStockphoto; B5.5.2 With God/Fotolia; B5.7.1 Martyn Chillmaid/Science
Photo Library; B7.2.1 Kamila Panasiuk/Fotolia; B7.8.1 Lea Paterson/
Science Photo Library; B7.8.3 Assembly/Getty Images; B8.4.1 CC Studio/
Science Photo Library; B8.5.1 Dr Kari Lounatmaa/Science Photo Library;
B8.6.1 Phototake Inc./Alamy; B9.1.1 Cordelia Molloy/Science Photo
Library; B9.1.2 SAPS; B9.2.4 Noel Hendrickson/Getty Images; B9.3.1
Chris Mattison/FLPA; B9.6.1 Steve Gschmeissner/Getty Images; B9.6.2
Martin Leigh/Oxford Scientific/Getty Images; B9.10.2 Volff/Fotolia; B10.2.1
Linn Currie/Shutterstock; B10.7.1 Look at Sciences/Science Photo
Library; B10.7.2 EVAfotografie/iStockphoto; B11.2.1 International Rice
Research Institute (IRRI); B11.2.1 Courtesy Golden Rice Humanitarian
Board. www.goldenrice.org; B12.3.1 De Agostini/Getty Images; B12.5.1
Roxana/Fotolia; B12.5.1 Lynwood Chase/Science Photo Library; B13.1.1
Jurgen and Christine Sohns/FLPA; B13.4.1 William Mullins/Science Photo
Library; B14.2.1 Hans Schouten/FN/Minden/FLPA; B15.3.1 Zoonar GmbH/
Alamy; B15.5.1 Sinclair Stammers/Science Photo Library; B16.5.1 Olga
Popova/Fotoli.

iGCSE Biology Contents

Maths skills

This feature highlights the maths skills that you will need for your Science exams with short, visual explanations.

 links

Links will tell you where you can find more information about what you are learning and how different topics link up.

Welcome to AQA Level 1/2 Certificate in Biology

This book has been written for you by very experienced teachers and subject experts. It covers everything you need to revise for your exams and is packed full of features to help you achieve the very best that you can.

Key words are highlighted in the text. You can look them up in the glossary at the back of the book if you are not sure what they mean.

 Where you see this icon, you will know that this topic also forms part of the AQA Level 1/2 Certificate in Science: Double Award.

➡ *These questions check that you understand what you're learning as you go along. The answers are all at the back of the book.*

Many diagrams are as important for you to learn as the text, so make sure you revise them carefully.

Study tip

Study tips give you important advice on things to remember and what to watch out for.

Practical

This feature helps you become familiar with key practicals. It may be a simple introduction, a reminder or the basis for a practical in the classroom.

At the end of each chapter you will find:

End of chapter questions

These questions will test you on what you have learned throughout the whole chapter, helping you to work out what you have understood and what you need to go back and revise.

And at the end of each unit you will find:

Examination-style questions

These questions are examples of the types of questions you will answer in your actual examination, so you can get lots of practice during your course.

You can find answers to the End of chapter and Examination-style questions at the back of the book.

Animal and plant cells

All living things are made of cells. Cells are small and can only be seen with microscopes. **Light microscopes** are used in schools. **Electron microscopes** magnify things thousands of times larger.

Most human cells are like most other animal cells and have structures in common. They have:

- a **nucleus** to control the cell's activities
- **genes** on **chromosomes** in the nucleus that carry the instructions for making protein
- **cytoplasm** where many chemical reactions take place
- a **cell membrane** that controls the movement of materials such as glucose and mineral **ions** in and out of the cell
- **mitochondria** where energy is released during aerobic respiration
- **ribosomes** where **protein synthesis** takes place.

> **1** *In which part of the cell is energy released during respiration?*

Plant and **algal cells** also have:

- a rigid **cell wall** made of **cellulose** for support
- **chloroplasts** that contain **chlorophyll** for photosynthesis; the chloroplasts absorb light energy to make food
- a **permanent vacuole** containing cell sap.

> **2** *What is the function of chloroplasts?*

Algae are simple aquatic organisms which have many features similar to plant cells.

Key points

- Most human cells are similar to most other animal cells and contain features common to all cells: a nucleus, cytoplasm, cell membrane, mitochondria and ribosomes.
- Plant and algal cells contain all the structures seen in animal cells as well as a cell wall. Many plant cells also contain chloroplasts and a permanent vacuole filled with sap.

Study tip

To improve your grade, practise labelling all types of cell. You need to know the functions of each part so write these on the diagram. For example, if you label a plant cell chloroplast, add a note to say 'chloroplasts contain chlorophyll which absorbs light for photosynthesis'. Facts about cells link to many of the other topics you must learn.

Study tip

Remember that not all plant cells have chloroplasts.
Don't confuse chloroplasts and chlorophyll.

⬭ links

Revise more on photosynthesis in 9.1 'Photosynthesis'.

Key words: light microscope, electron microscope, nucleus, gene, chromosome, cytoplasm, cell membrane, ion, mitochondria, ribosome, protein synthesis, algal cell, cell wall, cellulose, chloroplast, chlorophyll, permanent vacuole

Practical

Looking at cells

We can use a light microscope to look at onion cells and either *Elodea* or algal cells. All the cells have a cell wall, cytoplasm and a vacuole. *Elodea* and algal cells have chloroplasts for photosynthesis, but the onion cells do not.

> **3** *Onion cells do not look green. Explain why.*

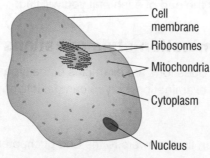

Figure 1 A simple animal cell like this shows the features which are common to all living cells – including human cells

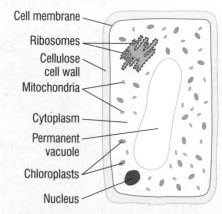

Figure 2 A plant cell has many features in common with an animal cell, as well as other features that are unique to plants

B1.2

Bacteria and yeast

- **Bacteria** are very small and can only be seen with a powerful microscope.
- Bacterial cells have a cell membrane and a cell wall which surround cytoplasm.
- Bacteria do not have a nucleus so the **genetic material** is found in the cytoplasm as a long strand of **DNA**.
- Some of the genes are located in circular structures called **plasmids**.
- When bacteria multiply they form a colony. **Bacterial colonies** can be seen with the naked eye.

> **1** *Where is the DNA found in a bacterial cell?*

- **Yeast** is a single-celled organism.
- Yeast cells have a nucleus, cytoplasm and a membrane surrounded by a cell wall.
- Yeast cells are specialised to survive with little oxygen. The cells can use **aerobic respiration** but when oxygen is not available they use **anaerobic respiration** (**fermentation**).
- Yeast cells reproduce by **asexual budding,** where a new cell grows out of the original one.
- Yeast can be useful in the production of ethanol and **antibiotics** and as a decomposer in food chains, but it may also break down stored food.

> **2** *What type of respiration is fermentation?*

Key points

- A bacterial cell consists of cytoplasm and a membrane surrounded by a cell wall. The genes are not in a distinct nucleus. Some of the genes are in circular structures called plasmids.
- Yeast is a single-celled organism. Each yeast cell has a nucleus, cytoplasm and a membrane surrounded by a cell wall.

Maths skills – Using units

1 km = 1000 m
1 m = 100 cm
1 cm = 10 mm
1 mm = 1000 μm (micrometres)

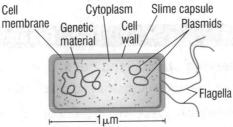

Figure 1 Bacteria come in a variety of shapes, but they all have the same basic structure

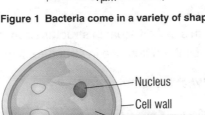

Figure 2 Yeast cells. These microscopic organisms have been useful to us for centuries.

Key words: bacteria, genetic material, DNA, plasmid, bacterial colony, yeast, aerobic respiration, anaerobic respiration, fermentation, asexual budding, antibiotic

B1.3 Specialised cells

Key points

- Cells may be specialised to carry out a particular function.
- Examples of specialised cells are fat cells, cone cells, root hair cells and sperm cells.
- Cells may be specialised to work as tissues, organs or whole organisms.

⬯ links

Revise more on the organisation of specialised cells into tissues, organs and organ systems in 2.4 'Cell growth and cancer' and 2.5 'Tissues and organs'.
Revise more on osmosis in 1.5 'Osmosis' and active transport in 1.6 'Active transport'.

There are many types of animal and plant cell. As an organism matures, each cell develops into a particular type. Some cells work individually while others are adapted to work as part of a tissue, an organ or whole organism. The structure of the cell is linked to its function:

- If a cell has many mitochondria, it must need a lot of energy, e.g. muscle cell, sperm cell.
- If a cell has many ribosomes, it is making a lot of protein, e.g. gland cells which produce enzymes.
- Cells with tails are able to move, e.g. **sperm** cells.

▶ **1** *Why do muscle cells need a lot of mitochondria?*

- Receptor cells have special structures which enable them to detect stimuli, e.g. the cone cells in the eye are light sensitive and are **specialised** to connect with the **optic nerve**.
- Plant cells with many chloroplasts will be photosynthesising, e.g. mesophyll cells of a leaf.
- **Root hair cells** increase the surface area of the root so that it can absorb water and **mineral ions** efficiently. Root hair cells are close to **xylem tissue** that transports water and mineral ions through the plant.

▶ **2** *What is the function of a root hair?*

Practical

Observing specialised cells

We can see different specialised cells under the microscope.

You could find illustrations in textbooks or on the internet.

Ask yourself:
- how is this cell different in structure from a generalised cell?
- how does the difference in structure help the cell to carry out its function?

▶ **3** *What is a generalised cell?*

Nucleus — Root hair — Large permanent vacuole

Middle section – full of mitochondria — Acrosome — Nucleus — Tail

Figure 1 A root hair cell

Figure 2 A sperm cell

Key words: sperm, specialised, optic nerve, root hair cell, mineral ion, xylem tissue

B1.4 Diffusion

Key points

- Diffusion is the net movement of particles from an area where they are at a high concentration to an area where they are at a lower concentration, down a concentration gradient.
- The greater the difference in concentration, the faster the rate of diffusion.
- Dissolved substances such as glucose and gases such as oxygen move in and out of cells by diffusion.

- Molecules in gases and liquids move around randomly because of the energy they have.
- **Diffusion** is the spreading out of the particles of a gas, or of any substance in solution (a **solute**).
- The **net movement** into or out of cells depends on the concentration of the particles on each side of the cell membrane.
- Because the particles move randomly, there will be a net (overall) movement from an area of *high concentration* to an area of *lower concentration*.
- The difference in concentration between two areas is called the **concentration gradient**.
- The larger the difference in concentration, the faster the rate of diffusion.

> **1** *What determines the net movement of particles across a cell membrane?*

Examples are:
- the diffusion of oxygen and glucose into the cells of the body from the bloodstream for **respiration**
- the diffusion of carbon dioxide into actively photosynthesising plant cells
- the diffusion of **simple sugars** and amino acids from the gut through cell membranes.

> **2** *Give an example of a gas which diffuses into leaves in bright sunlight.*

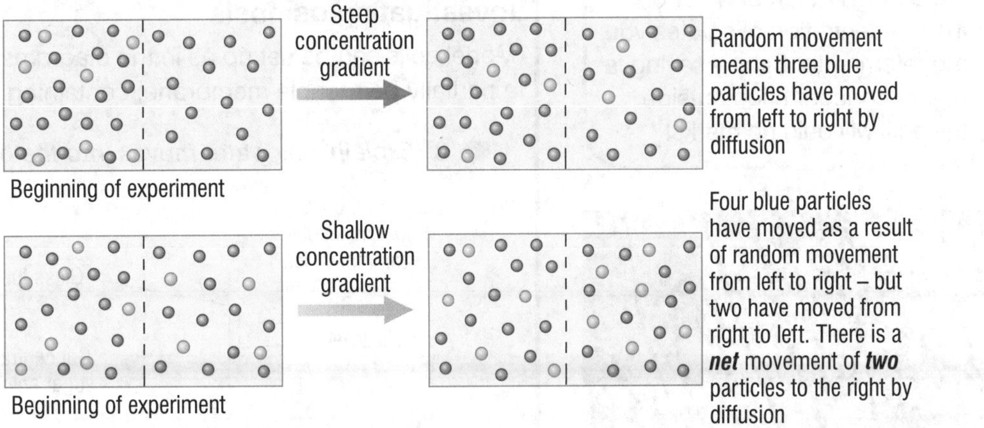

Study tip

Particles move randomly, but the net movement is from a region of high concentration to a region of low concentration.

Diffusion and osmosis are very important processes in living organisms. Remember that diffusion can refer to any moving particles, but osmosis refers to the movement of water.

Always make it clear in which direction there is net movement.

Both types of particles can pass through this membrane – it is freely permeable

Beginning of experiment

Steep concentration gradient

Random movement means three blue particles have moved from left to right by diffusion

Beginning of experiment

Shallow concentration gradient

Four blue particles have moved as a result of random movement from left to right – but two have moved from right to left. There is a *net* movement of *two* particles to the right by diffusion

Figure 1 This diagram shows the effect of concentration on the rate of diffusion. This is why so many body systems are adapted to maintain steep concentration gradients.

Key words: diffusion, solute, net movement, concentration gradient, respiration, simple sugars

Osmosis

- **Osmosis** is the movement of water.
- Just like diffusion, the movement of water molecules is random and requires no energy from the cell.
- Osmosis is the diffusion of water across a **partially permeable membrane**.
- The water moves from a region of high water concentration (a **dilute** solution) to a region of lower water concentration (a more **concentrated** solution).
- The cell membrane is partially permeable.

> **1** *What type of membrane is the cell membrane?*

Special scientific terms are used to compare the concentrations of two solutions.
- If the two solutions have the same concentrations, they are **isotonic**.
- The solution which is more concentrated (more solute and has relatively less water) is **hypertonic**.
- The solution which is more dilute (less solute and has relatively more water) is **hypotonic**.

> **2** *What term is used to refer to two solutions with identical concentrations?*

- When plant cells are placed in hypertonic solutions in a laboratory, a lot of water leaves the cell. The vacuole and cytoplasm shrink, then the membrane pulls away from the cell wall. This is referred to as **plasmolysis**.

Key points

- Osmosis is a special case of diffusion. It is the movement of water from a dilute to a more concentrated solution through a partially permeable membrane that allows water to pass through.
- Differences in the concentrations of solutions inside and outside a cell cause water to move into or out of the cell by osmosis.
- Osmosis is important to maintain turgor in plant cells. Animal cells can be damaged if the concentrations inside and outside the cells are not kept the same.

Study tip

When writing about osmosis, be careful to specify whether it is the concentration of water or the concentration of solutes you are referring to. Simply saying 'a higher concentration outside the cell' will gain no marks!

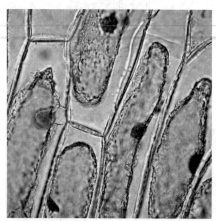

Figure 1 Plasmolysed plant cells in a concentrated solution

Key words: osmosis, partially permeable membrane, isotonic, hypertonic, hypotonic, plasmolysis

Practical

Investigating osmosis

Model cells can be set up as in the diagrams. The model cells are bags, made of a partially permeable membrane, containing a solution.

> **3** *Explain why water moves into the bag in (a) and out of the bag in (b).*

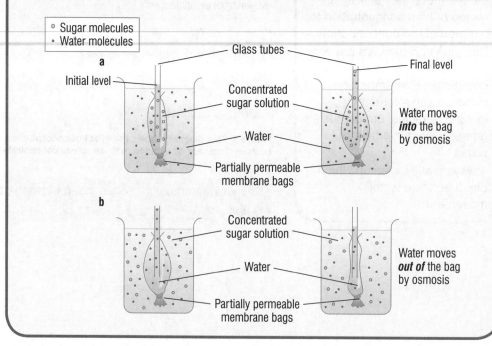

B1.6 # Active transport

Key points

- Substances are sometimes absorbed against (up) a concentration by active transport.
- Active transport uses energy from respiration.
- Cells can absorb ions from very dilute solutions, and actively absorb substances such as sugar and salt against a concentration gradient, using active transport.

◯◯ **links**

Revise more on the absorption of glucose in the gut in 5.6 'The digestive system', and on the absorption of solutes in the kidney in 7.3 'The human kidney'.

- Cells may need to absorb substances which are in short supply, i.e. against the concentration gradient.
- Cells use **active transport** to absorb substances across partially permeable membranes against the concentration gradient.
- Active transport requires the use of energy released in respiration.

▶ **1** *Why does active transport require energy?*

- Cells are able to absorb ions from dilute solutions. For example, root cells absorb mineral ions from the dilute solutions in the soil by active transport.
- Glucose can be reabsorbed in the **kidney tubules** by active transport.

▶ **2** *Name a substance which is moved into plants from soil by active transport.*

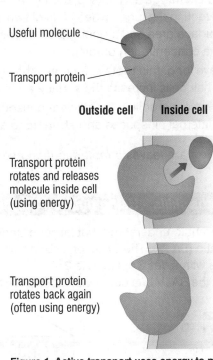

Figure 1 Active transport uses energy to move substances against a concentration gradient

Study tip

Do not refer to movement *along* a concentration gradient. Always refer to movement as *down* a concentration gradient (from high to low) for diffusion or osmosis, and as *against* a concentration gradient (from low to high) for active transport.

Key words: active transport, kidney tubules

Exchanging materials

Key points

- Single-celled organisms have a relatively large surface area to volume ratio so all necessary exchanges with the environment take place over this surface.

- In multicellular organisms, many organs are specialised with effective exchange surfaces.

- Exchange surfaces usually have a large surface area and thin walls, which give short diffusion distances. In animals, exchange surfaces will have an efficient blood supply or, for gaseous exchange, be ventilated.

Materials such as oxygen and soluble food must be able to reach all cells. Waste materials must also be able to leave cells efficiently.

- Small organisms have a large surface area to volume ratio. Single-celled organisms are tiny and can gain enough of materials such as oxygen by diffusion through their surface.

- As organisms increase in size, their surface area to volume ratio decreases.

- Large, complex organisms have many cells which are not in contact with the environment, so they have special **exchange surfaces** to obtain all the food and oxygen they need.

- Efficient exchange surfaces have a large surface area, thin walls or a short diffusion path, and an efficient transport system – the blood supply in animals.

▸ **1** *Why do large organisms need specialised exchange surfaces?*

- **Gaseous exchange** surfaces in animals must be **ventilated**. Oxygen is absorbed by the **alveoli** in the lungs when air is drawn in during breathing. The alveoli have a large surface area and a good blood supply to carry the oxygen away and maintain a concentration gradient.

- Plants have long, thin roots to increase the surface area for water absorption. The root hair cells increase the surface area even more.

- Plant leaves are modified for efficient gaseous exchange. The leaves are flat and thin with internal air spaces and **stomata** to allow gases in and out of the leaves.

▸ **2** *How are leaves adapted to increase their surface area?*

⦾ links

You will use the idea of surface area to volume ratio when you revise the adaptations of animals and plants for living in a variety of different habitats in 12.1 'Adapt and survive' to 12.4 'Competition in animals'.

Maths skills – Using units

It is important to understand that larger organisms have a smaller surface area to volume ratio (SA:V). The SA:V of a cube with sides 1 cm long is 6:1. The SA:V for a cube with sides 3 cm long is 2:1.
Calculate the SA:V of a cube with sides 2 cm long.

1 cm
1 cm   1 cm
SA : V ratio = 6 : 1

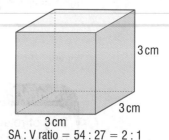
3 cm
3 cm
3 cm
SA : V ratio = 54 : 27 = 2 : 1

Study tip

Make sure you understand why the surface area to volume ratio decreases as the size of the organism increases. To gain full marks, learn the features of an exchange surface that makes exchange more efficient. SA:V is a very important concept in biology.

⦾ links

Revise more on the adaptations of plant leaves for diffusion and the exchange of materials in 9.4 'Exchange in plants'.

Key words: exchange surface, gaseous exchange, ventilated, alveoli, stomata

B1.8 Exchange in the gut

DOUBLE AWARD

Key points

- The villi in the small intestine provide a large surface area with an extensive network of blood capillaries.
- The villi mean the small intestine is well adapted as an exchange surface to absorb the products of digestion, both by diffusion and by active transport.

- The food we eat is digested in the **digestive system** into small, soluble molecules. In the **small intestine** these solutes are absorbed into the blood. The **villi** line the inner surface of the small intestine and are the exchange surface for food molecules.
- The villi are finger-like projections which greatly increase the surface area for absorption to take place.
- The walls of the villi are very thin and there are many capillaries close to the wall.

> **1** *Give two features of the villi which make them efficient exchange surfaces.*

- The soluble products of digestion can be absorbed into the villi by either diffusion or active transport.

> **2** *Suggest one substance which will pass from the gut to the blood.*

∞ links

Revise more on chemistry of carbohydrates, proteins and lipids as well as the breakdown of food in the digestive system in 3.1 'Carbohydrates, lipids and proteins' and 3.3 'Factors affecting enzyme action'.
Revise more on the structure of the whole of the digestive system in 2.5 'Tissues and organs'.
Revise more on glucose, amino acids, fatty acids and glycerol in 5.6 'The digestive system'.

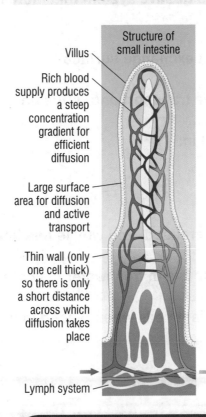

Villus

Rich blood supply produces a steep concentration gradient for efficient diffusion

Structure of small intestine

Large surface area for diffusion and active transport

Thin wall (only one cell thick) so there is only a short distance across which diffusion takes place

Lymph system

Figure 1 Thousands of finger-like projections in the wall of the small intestine – the villi – make it possible for all the digested food molecules to be transferred from your small intestine into your blood by diffusion and active transport

Study tip

Always relate the features of an exchange surface to its function. The two key examples to learn are alveoli (in the lungs) and villi (in the small intestine).

Key words: digestive system, small intestine, villi

1 **a** Name three structures which are found in plant cells but not animal cells.

    b Which of these three structures is not found in a yeast cell?

2 Why do some cells have a large number of ribosomes?

3 What is the difference between diffusion and osmosis?

4 What is meant by the term 'hypotonic'?

5 Name the structures in the human digestive system that increase the efficiency of the exchange surface.

6 What are the features of an efficient exchange surface?

7 Give two differences between active transport and diffusion.

8 Give an example of active transport in:

    a plants

    b a human.

9 How is the surface area of a root increased, and why is this important?

10 Explain why animals which normally live in freshwater may die if placed in sea water.

11 Explain in detail what happens to plant cells when placed in a hypertonic solution.

Chapter checklist

Tick when you have:

reviewed it after your lesson ✔ ☐ ☐

revised once – some questions right ✔ ✔ ☐

revised twice – all questions right ✔ ✔ ✔

Move on to another topic when you have all three ticks

	✔	✔	✔
Animal and plant cells	☐	☐	☐
Bacteria and yeast	☐	☐	☐
Specialised cells	☐	☐	☐
Diffusion	☐	☐	☐
Osmosis	☐	☐	☐
Active transport	☐	☐	☐
Exchanging materials	☐	☐	☐
Exchange in the gut	☐	☐	☐

B2.1

Cell division, growth and differentiation

Key points

- In body cells, chromosomes are found in pairs.
- Body cells divide by mitosis to produce more identical cells for growth, repair and replacement, or in some cases asexual reproduction.
- In plant cells, mitosis takes place throughout life in the meristems found in the shoot and root tips.
- Most types of animal cell differentiate at an early stage of development. Many plant cells can differentiate throughout their life.

Study tip

Cells produced by mitosis are genetically identical.

⚭ links

Revise more on alleles in 10.5 'Inheritance in action' and on the results of differentiation in 2.5 'Tissues and organs'.

- Cell division is necessary for the growth of an organism, or for the repair of damaged tissues.
- **Mitosis** results in two identical cells being produced from the original cell.
- Chromosomes, which look like threads, contain the genes (**alleles**) which must be passed on to each new cell.
- A copy of each chromosome is made before the cell divides and one of each chromosome goes to each new cell.
- In early development of animal and plant embryos the cells are unspecialised and are called **stem cells**.
- Most animal cells differentiate early in development and cell division is mainly for repair and replacement.
- Some differentiated cells cannot divide so they are replaced by **adult stem cells** such as those found in the bone marrow.
- Plants cells can differentiate throughout the life of the plant as it continues to grow. Actively dividing plant tissues are called meristems.
- Cells of offspring produced by asexual reproduction are produced by mitosis from the parent cell. They contain the same alleles as the parents.
- Producing genetically identical offspring is known as **cloning**.

⟫ **1** *Which type of cell division produces two identical cells from the original cell?*

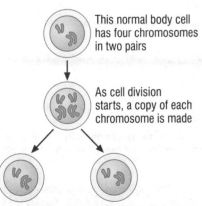

This normal body cell has four chromosomes in two pairs

As cell division starts, a copy of each chromosome is made

The cell divides in two to form two daughter cells. Each daughter cell has a nucleus containing four chromosomes identical to the ones in the original parent cell.

Figure 1 Two identical cells are formed by the simple division that takes place during mitosis. For simplicity, this cell is shown with only two pairs of chromosomes (there are actually 23 pairs).

Practical

Observing mitosis

⟫ **2** *Look at the photograph of an onion root tip. How can you identify chromosomes?*

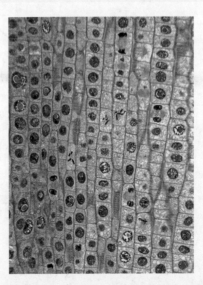

Key words: mitosis, alleles, stem cell, adult stem cell, cloning

B2.2 Cell division in sexual reproduction

- Cells in reproductive organs, e.g. testes and ovaries, divide by **meiosis** to form sex cells (gametes). In humans, the **gametes** are the sperm and **ova**.
- Each gamete has only one chromosome from each original pair. All of the cells are different from each other and the parent cell.
- Sexual reproduction results in variation as the gametes from each parent fuse. So half the genetic information comes from the father and half from the mother.
- When gametes join at fertilisation, a single body cell with new pairs of chromosomes is formed.
- A new individual then develops by this cell repeatedly dividing by mitosis.

▐▶ **1** *What type of cells are produced by meiosis?*

Meiosis

- Before division, a copy of each chromosome is made.
- The cell now divides twice to form four gametes (sex cells).
- Each gamete has a single set of chromosomes each with a different combination of genes.

▐▶ **2** *Explain how four gametes are formed from one cell during meiosis.*

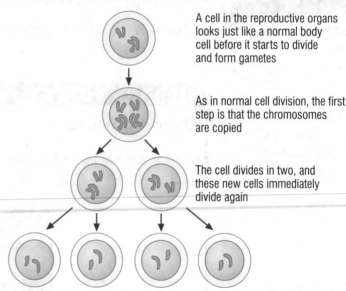

A cell in the reproductive organs looks just like a normal body cell before it starts to divide and form gametes

As in normal cell division, the first step is that the chromosomes are copied

The cell divides in two, and these new cells immediately divide again

This gives four sex cells, each with a single set of chromosomes – in this case two instead of the original four

Figure 1 The formation of sex cells in the ovaries and testes involves meiosis to halve the chromosome number. The original cell is shown with only two pairs of chromosomes, to make it easier to follow what is happening.

Key words: meiosis, gametes, ova

Key points

- Cells in the reproductive organs divide by meiosis to form the gametes (sex cells).
- Body cells have two sets of chromosomes; gametes have only one set.
- In meiosis, the genetic material is copied and then the cell divides twice to form four gametes, each with a single set of chromosomes.
- Sexual reproduction gives rise to variety because genetic information from two parents is combined.

Study tip

Make sure you can spell 'mitosis' and 'meiosis' correctly and learn the stages of the two types of cell division. Make a list to show when organisms use mitosis or meiosis (e.g. types of reproduction).

Don't confuse the two types of cell division.

Mitosis = making identical two.

Meiosis = making eggs (and sperm).

Student Book
pages 24–25

B2.3

Stem cells

- Stem cells are unspecialised cells which are found in the human embryo and adult bone marrow.
- An embryo is formed when an egg and sperm fuse to form a **zygote** and this cell divides many times to form a ball of cells. The inner layers of the ball are **embryonic stem cells**.
- Layers of cells in the embryo differentiate into all the cells the body needs.
- When stem cells change into all the different types of body cell, e.g. nerve cells or muscle cells, we say the cells differentiate.

> 1 *What do we mean by 'differentiate'?*

- **Adult stem cells** in the bone marrow can change into other types of cell, e.g.13blood cells.
- It is hoped that human stem cells can be made to differentiate into many types of cell. The cells formed could then be used to treat conditions such as paralysis, e.g. by differentiating into new nerve cells. This area of research is called **therapeutic cloning** and has already been successful in producing new organs such as a **trachea**.

> 2 *Where are stem cells found in adult humans?*

Key points

- Embryonic stem cells (from human embryos) and adult stem cells (from adult bone marrow) can be made to differentiate into many different types of cell.
- Stem cells have the potential to treat previously incurable conditions. We may be able to grow nerve cells to cure paralysis or whole new organs for people who need them.

Key words: zygote, embryonic stem cell, adult stem cell, therapeutic cloning, trachea

---

Student Book
pages 26–27

B2.4

Cell growth and cancer

Normal, healthy cells divide in a set sequence called the **cell cycle**. There are periods of active cell division followed by a non-dividing phase. In embryos and young, rapidly growing people the active periods are more frequent. After **puberty**, the cell cycle slows down in most tissues. Some tissues such as skin, blood and the lining of the digestive system, continue to replace cells.

Tumours

The process of mitosis is normally well controlled. However, sometimes a cell will change, due to mutations in the genetic material, and start to divide in an uncontrolled way.

- A mass of abnormally growing cells is called a **tumour**.
- A **benign tumour** grows in one place. Although it does not invade other tissues, it can be dangerous if it grows in tissue such as in the brain and compresses it.
- **Malignant tumours** can spread (**metastase**) to healthy tissue and are the ones we call **cancer**.
- Some malignant cells may enter the bloodstream and circulate to other parts of the body, forming secondary tumours.

> 1 *What is a tumour?*

Key points

- Tumours result from the abnormal, uncontrolled growth of cells.
- Benign tumours form in one place and do not spread to other tissues.
- Malignant tumours invade healthy tissue and may spread to other healthy tissues in the bloodstream to form secondary tumours.
- Tumours can be caused by a number of factors, including chemical carcinogens and ionising radiation.

Causes of cancer

- **Carcinogens** are cancer-causing chemicals. These include asbestos and the chemicals found in tobacco smoke.
- **Ionising radiation**, such as UV light and X-rays, can cause cancer tumours to form.

> 2 *What are the main causes of cancer?*

Key words: cell cycle, puberty, tumour, benign tumour, malignant tumour, metastase, cancer, carcinogens, ionising radiation

B2.5

Tissues and organs

Key points

- A tissue is a group of cells with similar structure and function.
- Organs are made of tissues. One organ may contain several types of tissue.
- Animal organs include the stomach and heart.
- Plant organs include stems, roots and leaves.

⬭ links

Revise more on specialised cells in 2.1 'Cell division, growth and differentiation'.
Revise more on the structure of the leaf in 9.4 'Exchange in plants'.

Key words: multicellular organism, differentiate, tissue, muscular tissue, glandular tissue, epithelial tissue, epidermal tissue, palisade mesophyll, spongy mesophyll, xylem, phloem, organ, digestive juices

Tissues

During the development of **multicellular organisms** the cells **differentiate**. Different cells have different functions. A **tissue** is a group of cells with similar structure and function. Animal tissues include:

- **muscular tissue**, which can contract to bring about movement
- **glandular tissue**, to produce substances such as enzymes or hormones
- **epithelial tissue**, which covers some parts of the body.

⫸ **1** *What does glandular tissue produce?*

Plant tissues include:

- **epidermal tissue**, which covers the plant
- **palisade mesophyll**, which contains many chloroplasts and can photosynthesise
- **spongy mesophyll**, which has some chloroplasts, many air spaces between the cells and a large surface area for diffusion of gases
- **xylem** and **phloem**, which transport substances around the plant.

⫸ **2** *What is the function of palisade tissue?*

Organs

Organs are made up of tissues. The **stomach** is an organ made up of:
- muscular tissue to churn the stomach contents
- glandular tissue to produce **digestive juices**
- epithelial tissue to cover the outside and the inside of the stomach.

The **leaf**, **stem** and **root** are plant organs which contain epidermal tissue, mesophyll, xylem and phloem.

Study tip

Remember that both plants and animals have organs. You should know the tissues that make up the stomach and the tissues in plant organs such as the leaf, stem and root. Always relate the structure of an organ to its function.

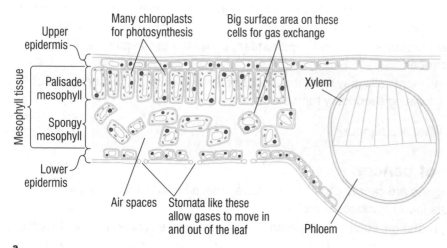
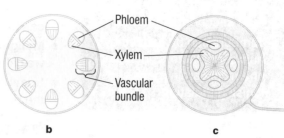

a

Figure 1 Plants have specific tissues to carry out particular functions. They are arranged in organs such as the **a** leaf, **b** stem and **c** roots.

B2.6 Organ systems

Multicellular organisms are made up of **organ systems** which work together. Each organ system is made up of several organs that work together to perform a particular function.

The **digestive system** is responsible for changing the food you eat from **insoluble molecules** into soluble molecules and absorbing them into the blood.

The digestive system is a **muscular tube** which includes:

● glands, such as the **pancreas** and **salivary glands** which produce digestive juices containing **enzymes**

▐▐▶ **1 What are enzymes?**

● the stomach and small intestine where digestion occurs
● the liver which produces bile
● the small intestine where the absorption of soluble food occurs
● the large intestine where water is absorbed from the undigested food, producing faeces.

▐▐▶ **2 Where is soluble food absorbed?**

Key points

● Organ systems are groups of organs that perform a particular function.
● The digestive system in a mammal is an example of a system where substances are exchanged with the environment.

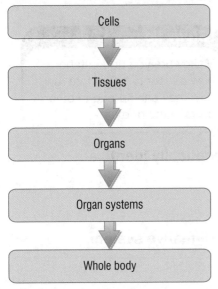

Figure 1 Larger multicellular organisms have many levels of organisation

Cells → Tissues → Organs → Organ systems → Whole body

○○ links

Revise more on the adaptations of the villi in the small intestine as an exchange surface in 1.8 'Exchange in the gut'.

Revise more on the role of the liver and bile in the digestion of food in 5.7 'Making digestion efficient'.

Study tip

Make sure you know the meanings of all the key words in this chapter. These biological terms are important in most topics.

Key words: organ system, digestive system, insoluble molecule, muscular tube, pancreas, salivary gland, enzyme

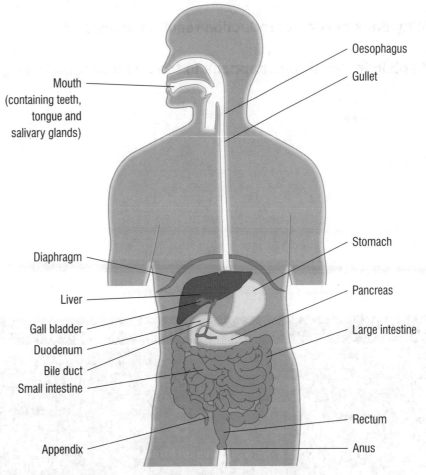

Figure 2 The main organs of the human digestive system

Labels: Mouth (containing teeth, tongue and salivary glands), Oesophagus, Gullet, Diaphragm, Stomach, Liver, Pancreas, Gall bladder, Large intestine, Duodenum, Bile duct, Small intestine, Appendix, Rectum, Anus

1 Name three organs in the digestive system.

2 List the tissues found in a leaf.

3 What are alleles?

4 Which type of cell division produces two identical cells?

5 Name two sources of stem cells.

6 What is meant by 'differentiation of cells'?

7 What is meant by a 'malignant' tumour?

8 Which type of cell division produces gametes?

> **Study tip**
>
> Make sure you understand how cancer tumours form and how they can spread to other parts of the body.

9 Explain why offspring produced by asexual reproduction are genetically identical.

10 Why does sexual reproduction result in variation?

11 Explain in detail what happens to food as it passes through the digestive system.

Chapter checklist ✓✓✓

Tick when you have:

	☑	☐	☐
reviewed it after your lesson	☑	☐	☐
revised once – some questions right	☑	☑	☐
revised twice – all questions right	☑	☑	☑

Move on to another topic when you have all three ticks

Cell division, growth and differentiation	☐	☐	☐
Cell division in sexual reproduction	☐	☐	☐
Stem cells	☐	☐	☐
Cell growth and cancer	☐	☐	☐
Tissues and organs	☐	☐	☐
Organ systems	☐	☐	☐

B3.1

Carbohydrates, lipids and proteins

Carbohydrates

All **carbohydrates** are made up of units of sugar.

- Glucose has one unit of sugar. Sucrose has two units linked together. These are simple sugars.
- Starch and cellulose are made up of long chains of simple sugar units that are bonded together. These are **complex carbohydrates**.

Lipids

Lipids are molecules made up of three molecules of fatty acids linked to a molecule of glycerol.

> **1** *What is a complex carbohydrate?*

Proteins

Proteins are made up of long chains of **amino acids**. The long chains are folded to form a specific shape. Other molecules can fit into these specific shapes. If the protein is heated, the shape is changed and the protein is **denatured**.

Each protein has a specific function. Some proteins are structural components of tissues such as muscles. Other proteins are hormones, antibodies or enzymes.

> **2** *What happens to a protein molecule if it is heated?*

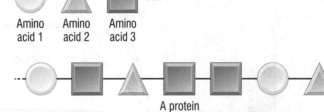

Figure 3 Amino acids are the building blocks of proteins. They can join in an almost endless variety of ways to produce different proteins.

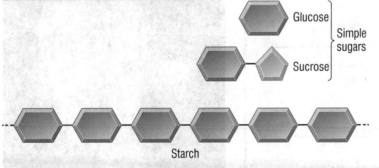

Figure 1 Carbohydrates are all based on a single simple sugar unit

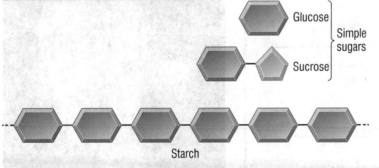
Glycerol

Figure 2 It is the combination of fatty acids joined to the glycerol molecule that affect the melting point of a lipid

Practical

Food tests

The main food groups can be identified using standard food tests.

- *Carbohydrates*: Iodine test for starch; Benedict's test for glucose.
- *Protein*: Biuret test.
- *Lipids*: Ethanol test.

> **3** *What results would you expect if you tested some egg white with* **a** *iodine solution,* **b** *Benedict's solution,* **c** *Biuret solution?*

Safety: Wear eye protection.

B3.2 Catalysts and enzymes

Key points

- Catalysts increase the rate of chemical reactions without changing chemically themselves.
- Enzymes are biological catalysts.
- Enzymes are proteins. The amino acid chains are folded to form the active site, which matches the shape of a specific substrate.
- The substrate binds to the active site and the reaction is catalysed by the enzyme.

- Chemical reactions in cells are controlled by proteins called enzymes.
- Enzymes are **biological catalysts** – they speed up reactions.
- Enzymes are large proteins and the shape of the enzyme is vital for its function. This shape has an area where other molecules can fit – the '**active site**'.
- The substrate in a reaction can be held in the active site and be either connected to another molecule or broken down.

Enzymes can:

- build large molecules from many smaller ones, e.g. building starch from glucose molecules
- change one molecule into another one, e.g. convert one type of sugar into another
- break down large molecules into smaller ones, e.g. all the digestive enzymes do this.

⟿ **1** *Name the area of a protein where other molecules can fit.*

Key words: catalyst, active site

Practical

Breaking down hydrogen peroxide

The effect of manganese(IV) oxide (a catalyst) and liver on the breakdown of hydrogen peroxide can be investigated.

⟿ **2** *Which is the better catalyst – catalase or manganese(IV) oxide? Use the graph to explain your answer.*

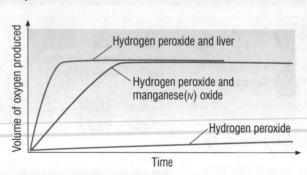

Figure 1 The decomposition of hydrogen peroxide to oxygen and water goes much faster using a catalyst such as manganese(IV) oxide. Raw liver contains the enzyme catalase, which speeds up the same reaction.

Study tip

Remember that the way an enzyme works depends on the shape of the active site that allows it to bind with the substrate.

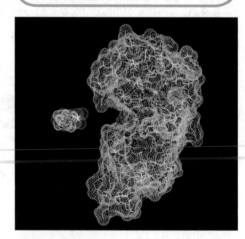

Figure 2 Enzymes are made up of chains of amino acids folded together to make large complex molecules, as you can see in this computer-generated image

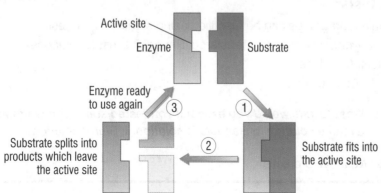

Figure 3 Enzymes act as catalysts using the 'lock-and-key' mechanism shown here

Student Book
pages 38–39

B3.3

Factors affecting enzyme action

Key points

- Enzyme activity is affected by temperature and pH.
- High temperatures denature the enzyme, changing the shape of the active site.
- pH can affect the shape of the active site of an enzyme and make it work very efficiently or stop it working.
- Digestive enzymes are produced by specialised cells in glands and in the lining of the gut. These enzymes work outside the body cells in the gut itself.

Study tip

Enzymes aren't killed (they are molecules found in living things, not living things themselves) – so make sure that you use the term 'denatured'.

- Enzyme reactions are similar to other reactions when the temperature is increased (up to a point).
- Reactions take place faster when it is warmer. At higher temperatures, the molecules move around more quickly and so collide with each other more often, and with more energy.
- However, if the temperature gets too hot, the enzyme stops working because the active site changes shape. We say that the enzyme becomes denatured.
- Each enzyme works best at a particular pH value. Some work best in acid conditions, such as the stomach, but others need neutral or alkaline conditions.
- If the pH is too acidic or alkaline for the enzyme, then the active site could change shape. Then the enzyme becomes denatured.

▶ **1** *What is meant by the term 'denatured'?*

Some enzymes work outside the body cells.

- Digestive enzymes are produced by specialised cells in glands and in the lining of the gut.
- The enzymes pass out of the cells and come into contact with the food so it is **digested**.
- Digestion involves the breakdown of large, insoluble molecules into smaller soluble molecules.

▶ **2** *What is meant by 'digestion'?*

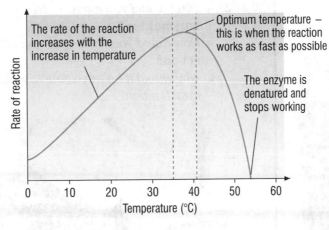

Figure 1 The rate of an enzyme-controlled reaction increases as the temperature rises – but only until the protein structure of the enzyme breaks down

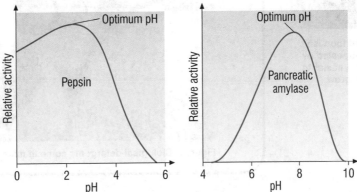

Figure 2 These two digestive enzymes need very different pH levels to work at their maximum rate. Pepsin is found in the stomach, along with hydrochloric acid, while pancreatic amalyse is in the first part of the small intestine along with alkaline bile.

⚭ links
Revise more on the different organs in the human digestive system in 2.5 'Tissues and organs' and 2.6 'Organ systems'.

Key word: digested

Student Book
pages 40–41

B3.4 Making use of enzymes

Key points

- Some microorganisms produce enzymes that pass out of the cells and can be used in different ways.
- People use biological detergents to remove stains from their clothes. They may contain proteases and lipases.
- Proteases, carbohydrases and isomerases are all used in the food industry.

Study tip

Remember that most enzyme names end in '–ase'.

Some enzymes used in industry work at quite high temperatures – so don't be put off if a graph shows an optimum temperature well above 45 °C!

Some microorganisms produce enzymes that pass out of their cells. These enzymes have many uses in industry but can be costly to produce.

- **Biological detergents** contain **proteases** and lipases that digest food stains. They work at lower temperatures than ordinary washing powders. This saves energy and money spent on electricity.
- Proteases are used to pre-digest proteins in some baby foods.
- **Isomerase** is used to convert glucose syrup into **fructose syrup**. Fructose is much sweeter, so less is needed in foods. The foods, therefore, are not so fattening.
- **Carbohydrases** are used to convert starch into sugar syrup for use in foods.
- In industry, enzymes are used to bring about reactions at normal temperatures and pressures. Traditional chemical processes require expensive equipment and a lot of energy to produce high temperatures and pressures.

▐▐▐➤ **1** *Which enzyme is used to convert glucose into fructose?*

Practical

Investigating biological washing powder

Weigh a chunk of cooked egg white and leave it in a strong solution of biological washing powder.

▐▐▐➤ **2** *What do you think will happen to the egg white? Explain your answer.*

▐▐▐➤ **3** **a** *What would you measure to see how effective the protease enzymes are?*

    b *How could you investigate the effect of surface area on enzyme action?*

    c *Why would it be advisable to wear disposable plastic gloves in this investigation?*

Figure 1 Learning to eat solid food isn't easy. Having some of it pre-digested by protease enzymes can make it easier to get the nutrients you need to grow.

Figure 2 Biological detergents come in many different forms

Key words: biological detergent, protease, isomerase, fructose syrup, carbohydrase

1. Name two factors that can alter the shape of an enzyme.

2. Name the two types of molecule which link together to form a lipid.

3. Name the molecules that bond together to form a protein.

4. List three functions of proteins.

5. What do we call the temperature at which an enzyme works best?

6. Why are proteases used in baby foods?

7. Give two types of reaction controlled by enzymes in cells.

8. Why does increasing the temperature increase the rate of a reaction?

9. Enzymes are catalysts but their rate of reaction only increases as the temperature is increased up to a point. Explain why.

10. Give one advantage and one disadvantage of using enzymes in industry.

11. Why do biological washing powders work more efficiently than non-biological powders?

Study tip

Remember that all organisms have enzymes. The optimum temperature for each of these may be different from human body temperature.

Analyse data carefully before answering enzyme questions. Practise reading graphs relating to enzyme activity.

Chapter checklist ✔ ✔ ✔

Tick when you have:

reviewed it after your lesson	✔	☐	☐	Carbohydrates, lipids and proteins	☐	☐	☐
revised once – some questions right	✔	✔	☐	Catalysts and enzymes	☐	☐	☐
revised twice – all questions right	✔	✔	✔	Factors affecting enzyme action	☐	☐	☐
Move on to another topic when you have all three ticks				Making use of enzymes	☐	☐	☐

1
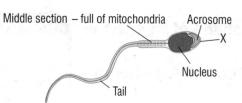
Middle section – full of mitochondria   Acrosome
X
Nucleus
Tail

   a What is structure X? *(1 mark)*

A sperm cell is adapted for its function.

   b **i** What is the function of the tail? *(1 mark)*

   ii Explain why a sperm cell has many mitochondria. *(2 marks)*

   iii The acrosome contains enzymes. What is the purpose of these enzymes? *(2 marks)*

   iv Which type of cell division produces the sperm? *(1 mark)*

   c In what way is the structure of a root hair cell:

   i the same as a sperm *(2 marks)*

   ii different from a sperm? *(2 marks)*

2 Cystic fibrosis is the UK's most common life-threatening inherited disease. In individuals who have the condition, the internal organs, especially the lungs and digestive system, become clogged with thick sticky mucus, resulting in chronic infections and inflammation in the lungs and difficulty digesting food.

The mucus covers the cells in the lungs and digestive system. Substances cannot cross the membranes easily.

   a Select the correct word or words from the box to complete the sentences.

active transport cytoplasm diffusion high impermeable low nucleus osmosis porous selectively permeable

The cells in the lung and digestive system are similar to all animal cells.
Surrounding the cell is a ＿＿＿＿＿＿ membrane.
Solutes or gases pass across this outer layer by a process of ＿＿＿＿＿ from a region of ＿＿＿＿＿ concentration and enter the ＿＿＿＿＿ inside the cell.
In the cell chemical reactions take place which require water.
Water enters the cell by a process called ＿＿＿＿＿ from a region of ＿＿＿＿＿ solute concentration. *(6 marks)*

   b People with cystic fibrosis have difficulty digesting food. Explain why. *(2 marks)*

   c Cystic fibrosis is a life-threatening condition. Explain why. *(5 marks)*

3 Some organisms live in environments that are very extreme, containing high levels of salt, high temperatures or high pressures. These organisms are called extremophiles.
Some extremophile bacteria can survive in very salty conditions.

   a Explain why most bacteria cannot survive in very salty conditions. *(3 marks)*

   b What would happen to the extremophiles if they were placed in river water. *(1 mark)*

Scientists were surprised to find extremophiles living in temperatures between 80°C and 105°C.

   c Explain why scientists did not expect to find bacteria in such high temperatures. *(2 marks)*

4 Describe how a tumour can spread from the skin to the liver. *(4 marks)*

Student Book
pages 44–45

B4.1 Breathing and gas exchange in the lungs

Key points

- The lungs are in your thorax. They are protected by your ribcage and separated from your abdomen by the diaphragm.
- The intercostal muscles contract to move your ribs up and out as the diaphragm flattens, increasing the volume of your thorax. The pressure decreases and air moves into your lungs.
- The intercostal muscles relax and the ribs move down and in, and the diaphragm domes up, decreasing the volume of your thorax. The pressure increases and air is forced out of your lungs.
- The alveoli provide a very large surface area and a rich supply of blood capillaries. This means gases can diffuse into and out of the blood as efficiently as possible.

- Moving air into and out of the lungs is called ventilating them or **breathing**.
- The lungs contain the exchange surface of the **respiratory (breathing) system**.
- The lungs are situated in the **thorax**, inside the ribcage and above the **diaphragm**, which separates the lungs from the **abdomen**.

When we breathe in:
- the **intercostal muscles**, between the ribs, contract moving the ribcage up and out
- the muscles of the diaphragm contract and the diaphragm flattens
- the volume of the thorax increases
- the pressure in the thorax decreases and air is drawn into your lungs.

When we breathe out:
- the diaphragm and the intercostal muscles of the ribcage relax
- the ribcage moves down and in and the diaphragm becomes domed
- the volume of the thorax decreases
- the pressure increases and air is forced out.

The movement of air in and out of the lungs is known as ventilation.

> ▶ **1** Which muscles contract when you breathe in?

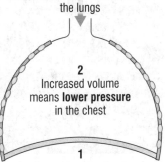

Breathing in

3 Atmospheric air at higher pressure than chest – so air is drawn into the lungs

2 Increased volume means **lower pressure** in the chest

1 As ribs move up and out and diaphragm flattens, the **volume** of the chest **increases**

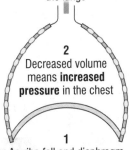

Breathing out

3 Pressure in chest higher than outside – so air is forced out of the lungs

2 Decreased volume means **increased pressure** in the chest

1 As ribs fall and diaphragm moves up, the **volume** of the chest **gets smaller**

Figure 1 Ventilation of the lungs

Adaptations of the alveoli

Your lungs are adapted to make gas exchange more efficient.
- Oxygen is absorbed by the lungs and carbon dioxide is removed from them.
- Efficient exchange surfaces have a large surface area, thin walls or a short diffusion path, and an efficient transport system.
- The lungs contain the gaseous exchange surface. The surface area of the lungs is increased by the alveoli (air sacs).
- The alveoli have thin walls, a large surface area and a good blood supply.
- The lungs are ventilated to maintain a steep diffusion gradient.
- Oxygen diffuses into the many **capillaries** surrounding the alveoli and carbon dioxide diffuses back out into the lungs to be breathed out.

> ▶ **2** Which structures increase the surface area of the lungs?

← Oxygen   ← Carbon dioxide   ← Air

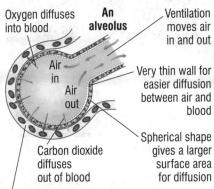

Oxygen diffuses into blood

An alveolus

Ventilation moves air in and out

Air in

Air out

Very thin wall for easier diffusion between air and blood

Carbon dioxide diffuses out of blood

Spherical shape gives a larger surface area for diffusion

Good blood supply – removes oxygen and brings carbon dioxide

Figure 2 The alveoli are adapted so that gas exchange can take place as efficiently as possible in the lungs

∞ links

Revise more on diffusion and concentration gradients in 1.4 'Diffusion'.

Key words: breathing, respiratory (breathing) system, thorax, diaphragm, abdomen, intercostal muscle, capillary

Student Book
pages 46–47

B4.2

Artificial breathing aids

Key points

- Different types of artificial breathing aids have been developed over the years to help people when they become paralysed by accident or disease and cannot ventilate their lungs.
- The different methods have advantages and disadvantages.

There are many reasons why someone cannot get enough oxygen into their bloodstream:

- If the alveoli are damaged, the surface area for gas exchange is reduced.
- If the tubes leading to the lungs are narrowed, less air can be moved through them.
- If the person is paralysed, their muscles will not work to pull the ribcage up and out.

> **1** *Sometimes insufficient oxygen reaches a person's bloodstream. Give one reason why.*

Several types of breathing aid have been developed:

- The 'iron lung' was used for people with polio who were paralysed. The person lay with their chest sealed in a large metal cylinder. When air was drawn out of the cylinder the person's chest moved out and they breathed in. The **vacuum** which was formed inside the cylinder created a **negative pressure**. When air was pumped back into the cylinder it created pressure on the chest and forced air out of the person's lungs.

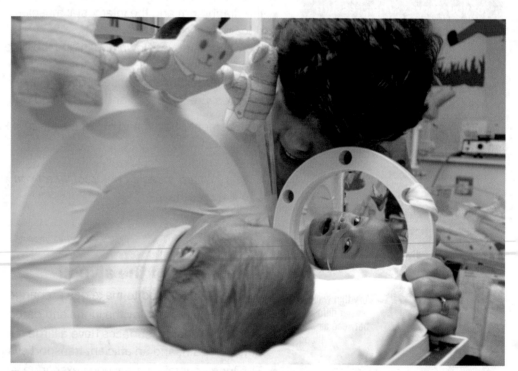

Figure 1 Without a negative pressure ventilator to draw air into its lungs, this child would have died

- Breathing aids which force measured amounts of air into the lungs use **positive pressure**. Bags of air linked to masks can force air down the trachea.
- Positive pressure aids are often smaller, easier to manage in the home and can be linked to computers for control.

> **2** *Give one example of a negative pressure breathing aid.*

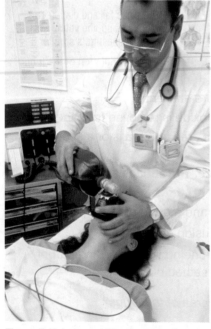

Figure 2 Using a positive pressure bag ventilator in an emergency situation saves many lives a year

Key words: vacuum, negative pressure, positive pressure

B4.3 Aerobic respiration

Aerobic respiration takes place continually in plants and animals. The process uses glucose and oxygen to release energy. Carbon dioxide and water are produced as waste products. Most of the chemical reactions of aerobic respiration take place in the mitochondria and are controlled by enzymes.

The equation for aerobic respiration is:

$$\text{glucose} + \text{oxygen} \rightarrow \text{carbon dioxide} + \text{water} \quad (+ \text{ energy})$$
$$C_6H_{12}O_6 + 6O_2 \rightarrow 6CO_2 + 6H_2O \quad (+ \text{ energy})$$

> **1** *Where does aerobic respiration take place in a cell?*

The energy released may be used by the organism to:

- build larger molecules from smaller ones
- enable muscle contraction in animals
- maintain a constant body temperature in colder surroundings in mammals and birds
- move materials such as mineral ions into cells against a concentration gradient (active transport)
- build sugars, nitrates and other nutrients into amino acids and then proteins in plants.

> **2** *Why is energy needed to make protein from amino acids?*

Key points

- Aerobic respiration involves chemical reactions that use energy.
- Most of the reactions in aerobic respiration take place inside the mitochondria.
- The energy released during respiration is used for many crucial life processes such as synthesis reactions for growth, active transport, movement, digestion, circulation and, in mammals and birds, maintaining body temperature.

Practical

Investigating respiration

Investigations involving aerobic respiration usually monitor the carbon dioxide produced. Limewater is used to detect carbon dioxide. The limewater turns cloudy. The quicker the limewater turns cloudy the faster carbon dioxide is being produced. It is also possible to detect a rise in temperature when respiration is occurring. If germinating peas are left in a thermos flask, the rise in temperature due to respiration can be monitored.

> **3** *Why don't we plan investigations to prove that oxygen is needed for aerobic respiration?*

Study tip

Make sure you know the word equation and balanced symbol equation for aerobic respiration.
Remember that aerobic respiration takes place in the mitochondria.

⚭ links

Revise more on active transport and the movement of mineral ions into root hair cells in 1.6 'Active transport', and on the use of energy in Chapter 16 'Energy and biomass in food chains and natural cycles'. There is also more about heat production and temperature control in 7.6 'Controlling body temperature'.

B4.4 | The effect of exercise on the body

- The energy that is released during respiration is used to enable muscles to contract.

- When exercising your muscles, you need an increased supply of glucose and oxygen, and you produce more carbon dioxide that has to be removed.

- Body responses to exercise include:
  - an increase in the heart rate, in the breathing rate and in the depth of breathing
  - glycogen stores in the muscles are converted to glucose for cellular respiration
  - the blood flow to the muscles increases.

- These responses act to increase the rate of supply of glucose and oxygen to the muscles and the rate of removal of carbon dioxide from the muscles.

- When you exercise, your muscles need more energy so that they can contract.

- You need to increase the rate at which oxygen and glucose reach the muscle cells for aerobic respiration. You also need to remove the extra waste carbon dioxide produced more quickly.

- The heart rate increases and the blood vessels supplying the muscles dilate (widen). This allows more blood containing oxygen and glucose to reach the muscles.

- Your breathing rate and the depth of each breath also increase. This allows a greater uptake of oxygen and release of carbon dioxide at the lungs.

- Muscles store glucose as **glycogen**. The glycogen can be converted back to glucose for use during exercise.

$$glucose + oxygen \rightarrow carbon\ dioxide + water \ (+ energy)$$
$$C_6H_{12}O_6 + 6O_2 \rightarrow 6CO_2 + 6H_2O \ (+ energy)$$

1 *Which sugar is needed by the muscles for aerobic respiration?*

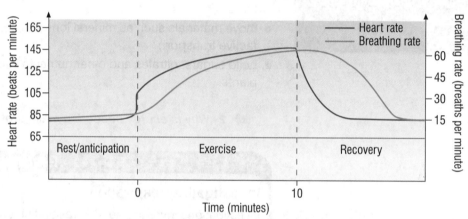

Figure 1 During exercise, the heart rate and breathing rate increase to supply the muscles with glucose and oxygen and to remove the extra carbon dioxide produced

	Unfit person	Fit person
Amount of blood pumped out of the heart during each beat at rest (cm³)	64	80
Volume of the heart at rest (cm³)	120	140
Resting breathing rate (breaths/min)	14	12
Resting pulse rate (beats/min)	72	63

Figure 2 The heart and lung functions change during exercise whether you are fit or not

2 *Use information from the table to describe the differences between a fit person and an unfit person.*

 Maths skills

When calculating a rate you must always refer to time.
You need to be clear about:
- the difference between the rate and the depth of breathing
- the difference between the breathing rate and the rate of respiration.

Many students will remember that if you exercise you will need more energy. Fewer students will remember that you will, therefore, need more oxygen and glucose. Very few will write about the need to remove more carbon dioxide. Make sure you write all the details needed.

Key word: glycogen

Student Book
pages 52–53 **B4.5** | # Anaerobic respiration

Key points

- If muscles work hard for a long time, they become fatigued and don't contract efficiently. If they don't get enough oxygen, they will respire anaerobically.

- Anaerobic respiration is respiration without oxygen. When this takes place in animal cells, glucose is incompletely broken down to form lactic acid.

- The anaerobic breakdown of glucose releases less energy than aerobic respiration.

- After exercise, oxygen is still needed to break down the lactic acid that has built up. The amount of oxygen needed is known as the oxygen debt.

- Anaerobic respiration in plant cells and some microorganisms results in the production of ethanol and carbon dioxide.

- If you use muscles over a long period, then they will get tired (fatigued) and stop contracting efficiently. For example, this might happen when you lift a weight repeatedly for a few minutes or go jogging.

- When your muscles cannot get enough oxygen for aerobic respiration, they start to respire anaerobically.

- The glucose is not completely broken down in **anaerobic respiration** and **lactic acid** is produced.

- Less energy is released from the glucose in anaerobic respiration.

- One cause of muscle fatigue is the build up of lactic acid.

- Blood flowing through the muscles removes the lactic acid.

> **1** *What is produced during anaerobic respiration in muscle cells?*

$$\text{glucose} \rightarrow \text{lactic acid} \quad (+ \text{ energy})$$
$$C_6H_{12}O_6 \rightarrow 2C_3H_6O_3 \quad (+ \text{ energy})$$

- When the exercise has finished, this lactic acid must be completely broken down. You still need to take in a lot of oxygen to do this.

- The extra oxygen needed is known as the **oxygen debt**. Eventually, the oxygen oxidises lactic acid into carbon dioxide and water.

$$\text{lactic acid} + \text{oxygen} \rightarrow \text{carbon dioxide} + \text{water}$$

Plants and microorganisms also respire anaerobically.

- Plant cells and yeast cells produce ethanol and carbon dioxide.

$$\text{glucose} \rightarrow \text{ethanol} + \text{carbon dioxide}$$
$$C_6H_{12}O_6 \rightarrow 2C_2H_5OH + \quad 2CO_2$$

- Some microorganisms, such as bacteria used in yoghurt production, produce lactic acid in anaerobic respiration.

Practical

Making lactic acid

Repeat a single action many times. For example, you could step up and down, lift a weight or clench and unclench your fist. You will soon feel the effect of a build up of lactic acid in your muscles.

> **2** *How can you tell when your muscles have started to respire anaerobically?*

Figure 1 Repeated movements can soon lead to anaerobic respiration in your muscles – particularly if you're not used to it

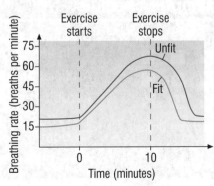

Figure 2 Hard exercise means everyone has to pay off their oxygen debt – but if you are fit you can pay it off faster!

Key words: anaerobic respiration, lactic acid, oxygen debt

1 What are the two waste products of aerobic respiration?

2 What is meant by 'anaerobic' respiration?

3 Which chemicals do muscle cells need more of during exercise?

4 What features of an alveolus makes it an efficient exchange surface?

Study tip

Always relate the features of an exchange surface to its function. The two key examples to learn are alveoli (in the lungs) and villi (in the small intestine).

5 Give three uses of energy released in respiration.

6 What is the chemical equation for anaerobic respiration in yeast cells?

7 Why do muscles become fatigued (tired) during vigorous exercise?

8 What changes occur to the breathing and heart rate during exercise?

9 Why do blood vessels in the muscles dilate during exercise?

10 Explain what is meant by an 'oxygen debt'.

11 Explain the sequence of events that draws air into the lungs.

12 Give one advantage of a positive pressure breathing aid compared with an iron lung.

Chapter checklist ✓ ✓ ✓

Tick when you have:

reviewed it after your lesson ✓ ☐ ☐

revised once – some questions right ✓ ✓ ☐

revised twice – all questions right ✓ ✓ ✓

Move on to another topic when you have all three ticks

Breathing and gas exchange in the lungs	☐	☐	☐
Artificial breathing aids	☐	☐	☐
Aerobic respiration	☐	☐	☐
The effect of exercise on the body	☐	☐	☐
Anaerobic respiration	☐	☐	☐

B5.1 The circulatory system and the heart

Key points

- The circulation system transfers substances to and from the body cells. It consists of the blood vessels, the heart and the blood.
- Human beings have a double circulation system.
- The heart is an organ that pumps blood around the body.
- The valves prevent backflow, ensuring the blood flows in the right direction through the heart.

Large organisms need a **transport system** to move materials around the body.

- Humans have a **blood circulation system** which consists of **blood vessels**, the **heart** and **blood**.
- The heart is a muscular organ that pumps blood around the body. It is actually two pumps held together.
- **Arteries** carry blood away from the heart. **Veins** carry blood to the heart.
- The right pump forces **deoxygenated** blood to the lungs where it picks up oxygen and loses carbon dioxide.
- After returning to the heart, the **oxygenated** blood is then pumped to the rest of the body by the left pump.
- The heart has four chambers. The upper ones called **atria** receive blood from the **vena cava** on the right and **pulmonary vein** on the left. The atria contract to move blood into the lower chambers, the **ventricles**. When the ventricles contract they force blood into the **pulmonary artery** from the right side and into the **aorta** on the left side. Valves in the heart prevent the blood from flowing in the wrong direction. The heart muscle is supplied with oxygenated blood via the **coronary arteries**.
- The action of the two sides of the heart results in a **double circulation**.

➡ **1** *What is the function of the valves in the heart?*

➡ **2** *What is meant by a 'double circulation'?*

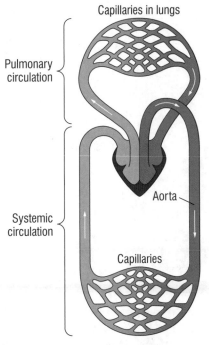

Figure 2 The two separate circulation systems supply the lungs and the rest of the body

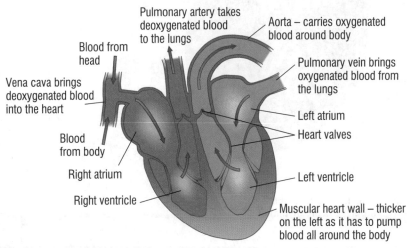

Figure 1 The structure of the heart

Study tip

Remember:
- arteries carry blood *away* from the heart and veins carry blood back to the heart – and this applies to the circulation system of the lungs as well
- the heart has *four* chambers
- ventricles pump blood *out* of the heart.

Key words: transport system, blood circulation system, blood vessel, heart, blood, artery, vein, deoxygenated, oxygenated, atria, vena cava, pulmonary vein, ventricle, pulmonary artery, aorta, coronary artery, double circulation

∞ links

Revise more on how digested food gets into the transport system in 1.8 'Exchange in the gut' and on how oxygen and carbon dioxide enter or leave the blood in 4.1 'Breathing and gas exchange in the lungs'.

Revise more on how oxygen is used in the cells and how carbon dioxide is produced in 4.3 'Aerobic respiration'.

Student Book
pages 58–59

B5.2

Helping the heart

Key points

- The resting heart rate is controlled by a group of cells in the right atrium that form a natural pacemaker.
- Artificial pacemakers are electrical devices used to correct irregularities in the heart rhythm.
- Artificial hearts are occasionally used to keep patients alive while they wait for a transplant, or for their heart to rest and recover.

- Adults have a natural resting heart rate of about 70 beats per minute. The natural resting heart rate is controlled by a group of cells that act as a **pacemaker**.
- The **natural pacemaker** is located in the right atrium in an area called the **sinoatrial node**.

> **1** *In which chamber of the heart is the natural pacemaker found?*

- Sometimes the rhythm of the heart becomes irregular if the natural pacemaker does not work properly.
- **Artificial pacemakers** are electrical devices that can be fitted in the chest to correct irregularities in the heart rate.
- If a person has a very weak or diseased heart, they may require a transplant. Donors are not always available so artificial hearts are being developed.

Artificial hearts can be used to:
- keep patients alive while waiting for a heart transplant
- allow the heart to rest as an aid to recovery.

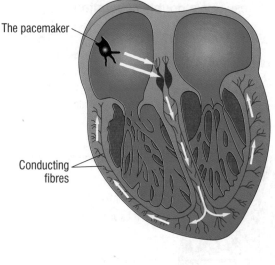

Figure 1 The pacemaker region of the heart, which controls the basic rhythm of your heart

The pacemaker

Conducting fibres

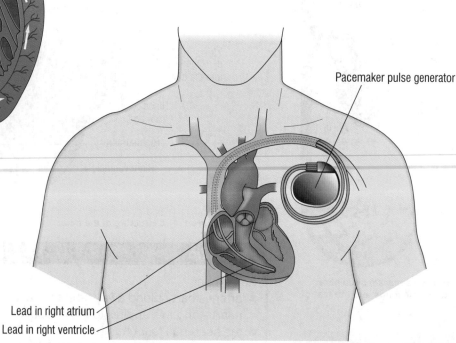

Pacemaker pulse generator

Lead in right atrium

Lead in right ventricle

Figure 2 An artificial pacemaker is positioned under the skin of the chest with wires running to the heart itself

∞ links
Revise more on heart disease in 5.3 'Keeping the blood flowing'.

Key words: pacemaker, sinoatrial node, artificial pacemaker

Keeping the blood flowing

Blood flows around the body in three main types of blood vessel: arteries, veins and capillaries.

Arteries:
- carry blood away from the heart
- have thick walls containing muscle and elastic tissue.

Veins:
- have thinner walls than arteries
- often have **valves** along their length to prevent the backflow of blood.

Capillaries:
- are narrow, thin-walled vessels
- carry the blood through the organs and allow the exchange of substances with all the living cells in the body.

Key points

- Blood flows round the body via the blood vessels. The main types of blood vessels are arteries, veins and capillaries.
- Substances diffuse in and out of the blood in the capillaries.
- Stents can be used to keep narrowed or blocked arteries open.
- Heart valves keep the blood flowing in the right direction.
- Damaged heart valves can be replaced by biological or mechanical valves.

Study tip

Make sure you can explain why a narrowed blood vessel or a leaky valve causes problems for a person's health.

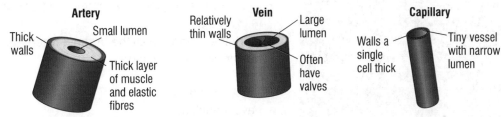

Artery — Thick walls, Small lumen, Thick layer of muscle and elastic fibres

Vein — Relatively thin walls, Large lumen, Often have valves

Capillary — Walls a single cell thick, Tiny vessel with narrow lumen

Figure 1 The three main types of blood vessels

▶ **1 What is the difference in structure between an artery and a vein?**

The heart keeps the blood flowing through the blood vessels. If blood vessels are blocked or too narrow, the blood will not flow efficiently. This will deprive the organs of nutrients and oxygen.

- **Stents** can be inserted to keep blood vessels open. This is particularly beneficial when a person has **coronary heart disease**. The disease causes coronary arteries to become narrowed due to fatty deposits, cutting off the blood supply to the heart muscle.
- Leaky valves mean the blood could flow in the wrong direction. Artificial or animal valves can be inserted in the heart to replace damaged valves.

▶ **2 Why are stents used?**

Study tip

Blood comes from the veins into the atria, through valves to the ventricles and then out via arteries.

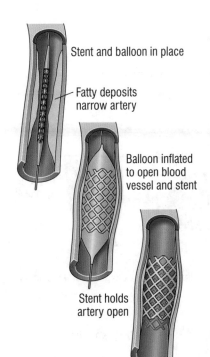

Stent and balloon in place

Fatty deposits narrow artery

Balloon inflated to open blood vessel and stent

Stent holds artery open

Figure 2 A stent being positioned in an artery

Practical

Blood flow

You can practise finding your pulse and look for the valves in the veins in your hands and wrists.

▶ **3 What does the pulse rate correspond to?**

Key words: valve, stent, coronary heart disease

Transport in the blood

Blood is a tissue. The fluid **plasma** contains **red blood cells**, **white blood cells** and **platelets**.

Blood plasma transports many substances including:

- carbon dioxide from the organs to the lungs
- soluble products of digestion from the small intestine to other organs
- **urea** from the liver to the kidneys where **urine** is made.

▕▶ **1** *Give an example of a gas transported by plasma.*

Red blood cells:

- are **biconcave discs** which do not have a nucleus
- contain the red **pigment** called **haemoglobin**
- use their haemoglobin to combine with oxygen, which forms **oxyhaemoglobin**, in the lungs
- carry the oxygen to all the organs, where the oxyhaemoglobin splits into haemoglobin and oxygen.

White blood cells:

- have a nucleus
- form part of the body's defence system against microorganisms.

Platelets:

- are small fragments of cells
- do not have a nucleus
- help blood to clot at the site of a wound.

▕▶ **2** *What is the function of platelets?*

Blood clotting is a series of enzyme-controlled reactions.

- The final reaction causes fibrinogen to change into fibrin.
- Fibrin forms a network of fibres trapping blood cells and forming a clot.
- The clot dries and forms a scab.

Key points

- Your blood plasma, with the blood cells suspended in it, transports dissolved food molecules, carbon dioxide and urea.
- Your red blood cells carry oxygen from your lungs to the organs of the body.
- Red blood cells are adapted to carry oxygen by being biconcave, which provides a bigger surface area, by containing haemoglobin, and by having no nucleus so more haemoglobin can fit in.
- White blood cells are part of the defence system of the body.
- Platelets are cell fragments involved in the clotting of the blood.
- Blood clotting involves a series of enzyme-controlled reactions that turn fibrinogen to fibrin to form a network of fibres and a scab.

Key words: plasma, red blood cell, white blood cell, platelet, urea, urine, biconcave disc, pigment, haemoglobin, oxyhaemoglobin

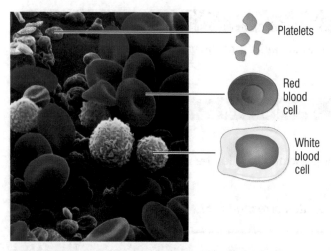

Figure 1 Red blood cells, white blood cells and platelets are suspended in the plasma

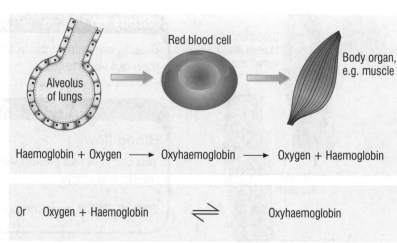

Haemoglobin + Oxygen ⟶ Oxyhaemoglobin ⟶ Oxygen + Haemoglobin

Or   Oxygen + Haemoglobin ⇌ Oxyhaemoglobin

Figure 2 The reversible reaction between oxygen and haemoglobin makes life as we know it possible by carrying oxygen to all the places where it is needed

The immune system and blood groups

Your **immune system** can detect foreign proteins which enter the body.

- **Antigens** are proteins on the surface of cells. Each person has a unique set of antigens.
- White blood cells respond to foreign antigens by producing **antibodies**.

Human blood groups

- Red blood cells have antigens on their surface. The most common antigens are antigen **A** and antigen **B**.
- In the plasma are antibodies **a** and **b**.

The ABO blood groups depend on the combination of antigens and antibodies.

Table 1 shows the combinations of antigens and antibodies that give the four ABO blood groups.

Blood group	Antigen on red blood cells	Antibody in plasma
A	A	b
B	B	a
AB	A and B	None
O	None	a and b

If blood group A is given to a person with blood group B, the antibody a will react with the antigen A of the donor blood and the blood cells will stick together (**agglutinate**). This can be fatal.

> 1 *Which blood group can be donated to people with any of the ABO groups?*

Organ transplants

- **Donor** organs have antigens on the surface of their cells.
- The **recipient** of the organ will produce antibodies that attack the donor antigens.
- This can result in the destruction of the donated organ and cause rejection.

The risk of rejection can be reduced by:

- matching the blood group and tissue type (similar antigens) of the donor as closely as possible to the recipient
- treating the recipient with **immunosuppressant drugs** to suppress the immune system.

> 2 *What type of drug reduces the risk of rejection of a donor organ?*

∞ links

Revise more on the structure of proteins in 3.1 'Carbohydrates, lipids and proteins'.

Key points

- Antigens are proteins on the surface of cells.
- There are four ABO blood groups – A, B, AB and O. These are based on the type of antigens on the surface of red blood cells and the type of antibodies in the blood plasma.
- In organ transplants, a diseased organ is replaced with a healthy one from a donor. The recipient's antibodies may attack the antigens on the donor organ as they do not recognise them.
- To prevent rejection of the transplanted organ, a donor organ with a similar tissue type to the recipient is used and immunosuppressant drugs are given that suppress the immune response.

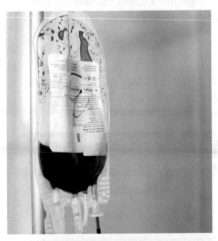

Donor	Recipient			
	A	B	AB	O
A	✓	✗	✓	✗
B	✗	✓	✓	✗
AB	✗	✗	✓	✗
O	✓	✓	✓	✓

(✓ = blood compatible; ✗ = blood incompatible and a transfusion would fail)

Figure 1 Mixing the wrong blood groups can cause agglutination and be fatal

Key words: immune system, antigens, antibodies, agglutinate, donor, recipient, immunosuppressant drug

Study tip

There are only TWO antigens in the ABO blood group system, A and B. AB has both and O has none. That is why no one reacts to O blood.

B5.6 The digestive system

The carbohydrates, proteins and lipids that you eat must be changed from insoluble molecules into soluble molecules. Only then can the soluble molecules be absorbed into the blood. The digestive system is responsible for this process.

The **digestive system** is a muscular tube which includes:

- glands, such as the pancreas and salivary glands which produce digestive juices
- the stomach and small intestine where digestion occurs due to the enzymes in the digestive juices
- the liver which produces bile to aid lipid digestion
- the small intestine where the absorption of soluble food occurs through the villi in the walls
- the large intestine where water is absorbed from the undigested food.

Undigested food forms the bulk of the faeces which leave the body via the anus.

> **1** *How is the small intestine adapted for efficient absorption of soluble molecules?*

Digestive enzymes are secreted from glands into the cavity of the gut. The insoluble food materials are mixed with the digestive juices by the squeezing action of the muscles of the gut. Each type of food is digested by a specific enzyme.

- **Amylase** (a carbohydrase) is produced by the salivary glands, the pancreas and the small intestine. Amylase catalyses the digestion of starch into sugars in the mouth and small intestine.
- **Protease** is produced by the stomach, the pancreas and the small intestine. Protease catalyses the breakdown of proteins into **amino acids** in the stomach and small intestine.
- **Lipase** is produced by the pancreas and small intestine. Lipase catalyses the breakdown of lipids (fats and oils) to **fatty acids** and **glycerol**.

> **2** *Which enzyme digests protein?*

The soluble food molecules diffuse into the blood from the intestine, down a steep concentration gradient. Some substances enter the blood by active transport.

Key points

- Digestion involves the breakdown of large insoluble molecules into soluble substances that can be absorbed into the blood across the wall of the small intestine.
- Digestive enzymes are produced by specialised cells in glands and in the lining of the gut.
- Carbohydrases, such as amylase, catalyse the breakdown of carbohydrates, such as starch, into sugars.
- Proteases catalyse the breakdown of proteins to amino acids.
- Lipases catalyse the breakdown of lipids to fatty acids and glycerol.

⬭ links

Revise more on moving substances in and out of cells in 1.4 'Diffusion', 1.5 'Osmosis' and 1.6 'Active transport'. Revise more on the adaptations of the gut for absorption in 1.8 'Exchange in the gut'.
Revise more on the structure of the digestive system in 2.5 'Tissues and organs' and 2.6 'Organ systems'.

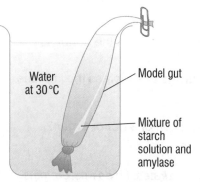

Figure 1 You can use this model gut to investigate the effect of temperature and pH on enzyme action

Water at 30 °C
Model gut
Mixture of starch solution and amylase

Key words: amylase, protease, amino acids, lipase, fatty acids, glycerol

Study tip

Learn three examples of digestive enzyme reactions.

Amylase	Starch → sugars
Protease	Protein → amino acids
Lipase	Lipids → fatty acids + glycerol

Practical

Investigating digestion

A model gut (see Figure 1) can be made using a special bag containing starch and amylase enzymes. The amylase breaks down the starch, and then soluble sugar leaves the model gut.

> **3** *Describe the chemical test and positive result for a starch, b a sugar.*

**Student Book
pages 68–69**

B5.7 | Making digestion efficient

Human digestive enzymes work best at body temperature, 37 °C, so the temperature in the gut is optimum. Different enzymes have different optimum pH values.

- Protease enzymes in the stomach work best in acidic conditions. Glands in the stomach wall produce hydrochloric acid to create very acidic conditions.
- Other proteases, amylase and lipase work best in the small intestine where the conditions are slightly alkaline.

Food leaving the stomach is very acidic so the pH must be changed. To do this the liver produces **bile** that is stored in the gall bladder and released into the small intestine when food enters.

Bile:
- neutralises the stomach acid
- makes the conditions in the small intestine slightly alkaline
- **emulsifies** fats (breaks large drops of fats into smaller droplets) to increase the surface area of the fats for lipase enzymes to act upon.

1 Why are fats emulsified?

Study tip

Make sure you know which enzymes are needed to digest each food type and how the pH conditions are altered as the food moves through the gut. To improve your grade, revise Chapter 3 together with 5.6 and 5.7.

Practical

Breaking down protein

The photograph shows what happened to similar-sized chunks of meat when placed in a) hydrochloric acid, b) pepsin (a protease from the stomach), and c) both pepsin and hydrochloric acid. The tubes were left for a few hours.

2 Explain the differences in the tubes after a few hours.

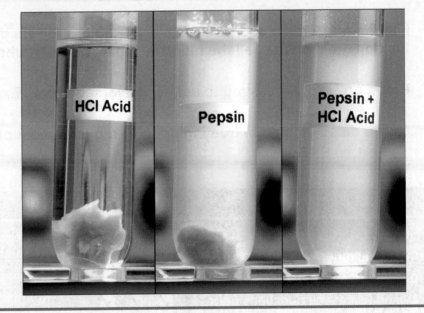

HCl Acid | Pepsin | Pepsin + HCl Acid

Study tip

You need to understand that bile does not contain enzymes. Bile is used to neutralise the stomach acid so that enzymes from the pancreas and small intestine have the correct pH. Bile also increases the rate of digestion of fat by increasing its surface area due to emulsification.

∞ links
Revise more on the sensitivity of enzymes to temperature and pH in 3.3 'Factors affecting enzyme action'.

Key words: bile, emulsify

1 Name the enzyme which digests starch.

2 Where is bile:

   a produced?

   b stored?

3 What prevents the backflow of blood in the veins?

4 Where does most digestion occur in the human gut?

5 Explain why proteins cannot be absorbed from the intestine.

6 What are the products of the digestion of:

   a proteins?

   b lipids?

7 Explain fully how bile helps in the digestion process.

8 What is the role of the pacemaker in the heart?

9 What is a stent and why is it used?

10 List the route the blood would travel from the body via the lungs and back to the body. Include the names of all the blood vessels and heart chambers.

11 Blood group O is referred to as the 'universal donor'. Explain why.

12 Give a disadvantage of treating people with immunosuppressant drugs.

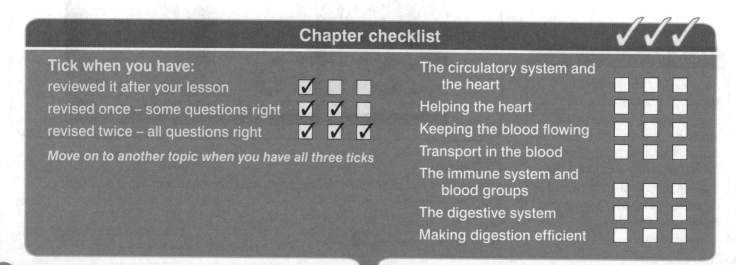

Chapter checklist ✓✓✓

Tick when you have:
reviewed it after your lesson ✓ ☐ ☐
revised once – some questions right ✓ ✓ ☐
revised twice – all questions right ✓ ✓ ✓

Move on to another topic when you have all three ticks

The circulatory system and the heart ☐ ☐ ☐
Helping the heart ☐ ☐ ☐
Keeping the blood flowing ☐ ☐ ☐
Transport in the blood ☐ ☐ ☐
The immune system and blood groups ☐ ☐ ☐
The digestive system ☐ ☐ ☐
Making digestion efficient ☐ ☐ ☐

B6.1 Responding to change and receptors

Key points

- The nervous system uses electrical impulses to enable you to react quickly to your surroundings and coordinate what you do.
- Cells called receptors detect stimuli (changes in the environment).
- Impulses from receptors pass along sensory neurones to the brain or spinal cord (CNS). The brain coordinates the response, and impulses are sent along motor neurones from the brain (CNS) to the effector organs.

- The **nervous system** has **receptors** to detect **stimuli**.
- The receptors are found in the **sense organs**: eye, ear, nose, tongue and skin.
- Light stimulates receptors in the eye and electrical **impulses** then pass to the brain along **neurones** (nerve cells). Other stimuli include sound, chemicals, temperature changes, touch and pain.
- The brain coordinates responses to many stimuli.

1 What stimuli are detected by the sense organs?

- The brain and spinal cord form the **central nervous system (CNS)**.
- **Nerves** contain neurones. **Sensory neurones** carry impulses from receptors to the CNS.
- **Motor neurones** carry impulses from the CNS to **effector organs,** which may be muscles or glands. The muscles respond by contracting. The glands respond by secreting (releasing) chemicals.

2 In what form do impulses pass along nerve cells?

The way your nervous system works can be summed up as:

receptor → sensory neurone → coordinator (CNS) → motor neurone → effector

Study tip

Be careful to use the terms neurone and nerve correctly. Talk about **impulses** (*not* messages) travelling along a neurone.

Sensory nerves carry impulses to the CNS. The information is processed and impulses are sent out along motor nerves to produce an action.

Sensory neurone cell body

Nerve endings in central nervous system

Motor neurone cell body

Nerve endings in a muscle or gland

Nerve fibre

Nerve fibre

Sensory receptor

Direction of impulse

Direction of impulse

Sensory neurone

Motor neurone

Figure 1 The rapid responses of our nervous system allow us to respond to our surroundings quickly – and in the right way!

Key words: nervous system, receptor, stimuli, sense organ, impulse, neurone, central nervous system (CNS), nerve, sensory neurone, motor neurone, effector organ

B6.2 Reflex actions

Key points

- Some responses to stimuli are automatic and rapid and are called 'reflex actions'. They involve sensory, relay and motor neurones.
- Reflex actions control everyday bodily functions, such as breathing and digestion, and help you to avoid danger.
- There are gaps between neurones called synapses. The release of chemicals into the synapse allows the impulse to cross from one neurone to another.

The main steps involved in reflex actions (**reflexes**) are:

- a receptor detects a stimulus (e.g. a sharp pin)
- a sensory neurone transmits the impulse to the CNS
- a relay neurone passes the impulse on
- a motor neurone is stimulated
- the impulse passes to an effector (muscle or gland)
- action is taken (the response).

1 *How does an impulse reach the CNS from a receptor?*

At the junction between two neurones is a **synapse**. Chemicals transmit the impulse across the gap.

The sequence from receptor to effector is a **reflex arc**.

2 *What is the function of a relay neurone?*

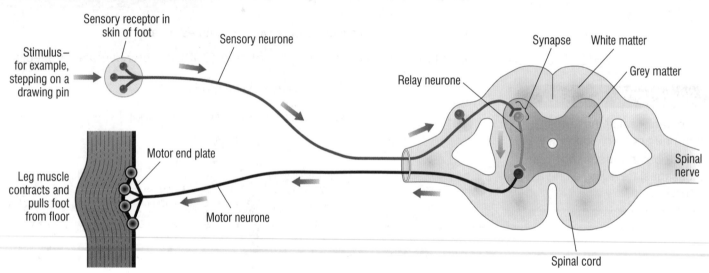

Figure 1 The reflex action which moves your foot away from a sharp object can save you from a nasty injury

Study tip

Learn the reflex pathway off by heart.

Stimulus → receptor → sensory neurone → relay neurone → motor neurone → effector → response.

Key words: reflex, synapse, reflex arc

B6.3

The brain

The brain:
- is made of billions of interconnected neurones
- receives impulses from sensory neurones all over your body and coordinates the responses
- controls complex behaviour and is responsible for your thoughts and feelings
- has different regions that carry out different functions.

Regions of the brain:
- The **cerebral cortex** is concerned with consciousness, intelligence, memory and language.
- The **cerebellum** is concerned mainly with the coordination of muscular activity.
- The **medulla** is concerned with unconscious activities, such as heartbeat and breathing.
- The **pituitary gland**, which produces **hormones**, such as ADH, is linked to the brain.

▶ **1** *Which region of the brain is mainly concerned with movement?*

Scientists have been able to map the regions of the brain to particular functions by:
- studying patients with brain damage
- electrically stimulating different parts of the brain
- using MRI scanning techniques to **monitor** brain activity after injury or when completing a task.

▶ **2** *What type of scanner can be used to monitor brain activity?*

Key points

- The brain is made of billions of interconnected neurones that control complex behaviour.
- It has different regions, for example the cerebral cortex, the cerebellum and the medulla, that each have different functions.
- Scientists map regions of the brain to their functions by studying patients with brain damage, by electrically stimulating different areas of the brain and by using MRI scanning techniques.

Study tip

Remember what each part of the brain controls:
- Cerebral cortex – memory and thought
- Cerebellum – movement
- Medulla – heartbeat and breathing.

∞ links

Revise more on the pituitary gland and one of the hormones it produces in 7.3 'The human kidney'. Revise more on thermoregulation in 7.6 'Controlling body temperature'.

Key words: cerebral cortex, cerebellum, medulla, pituitary gland, hormone, monitor

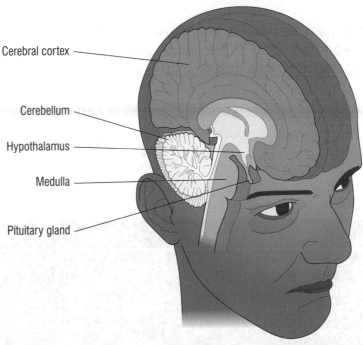

Cerebral cortex

Cerebellum

Hypothalamus

Medulla

Pituitary gland

Figure 1 The brain is very complex and coordinates and controls much of our behaviour

1 Name three external stimuli that affect humans.

2 Name the two types of effector found in the body and state how they respond to stimuli.

3 How are impulses passed across a synapse?

4 What is a reflex action?

5 Which region of the brain is concerned with memory and thought?

6 Why are reflex actions important?

> **Study tip**
>
> Learn the sequence of a reflex action. Whatever the example, the sequence of events is always the same. Don't panic if the situation is new to you. Identify the stimulus and response and then apply your knowledge.

7 Name two unconscious processes which are controlled by the medulla.

8 Give two methods that scientists use to find out which part of the brain performs particular functions.

9 Give the receptor for each of the following stimuli:

    a changes in position

    b chemicals

    c pressure.

10 List the stages of the pathway involved in a reflex action.

11 During a reflex action a synapse links the relay and motor neurones. Another neurone is also stimulated at the same synapse, which links directly with the brain. Suggest the importance of this link.

12 A man who suffered burns to the skin can no longer feel pain in that region. Explain why.

Chapter checklist ✓ ✓ ✓

Tick when you have:				Responding to change and receptors			
reviewed it after your lesson	✓	☐	☐		☐	☐	☐
revised once – some questions right	✓	✓	☐	Reflex actions	☐	☐	☐
revised twice – all questions right	✓	✓	✓	The brain	☐	☐	☐

Move on to another topic when you have all three ticks

1 a Which of the following is a reflex action? Tick all boxes that apply.   *(3 marks)*

Picking up a piece of paper from the floor. ☐

Pulling hand away from a very hot plate. ☐

Blinking when a bright light is shone in the eyes. ☐

Choosing a cake from a plate. ☐

Coughing when a crumb enters the trachea. ☐

b Give an example of a reflex action which occurs inside your body.   *(1 mark)*

c What is the main advantage of reflex actions?   *(1 mark)*

d Which part of the brain is concerned with intelligence and memory?   *(1 mark)*

2 The heart pumps blood around the body. This causes blood to leave the heart at high pressure.

The graph shows blood pressure measurements for a person at rest. The blood pressure was measured in an artery and in a vein.

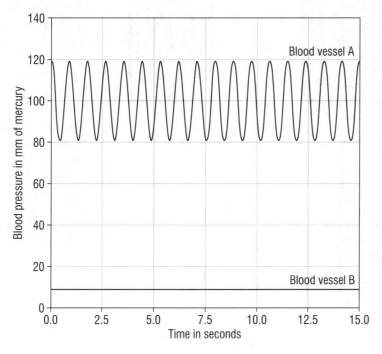

a Which blood vessel, **A** or **B**, is the artery?

Give **two** reasons for your answer.   *(2 marks)*

b Use information from the graph to answer these questions.

i How many times did the heart beat in 15 seconds?   *(1 mark)*

ii Use your answer from part **b i** to calculate the person's heart rate per minute.   *(1 mark)*

c During exercise, the heart rate increases. This supplies useful substances to the muscles and removes waste materials from the muscles at a faster rate.

i Name **two** useful substances that must be supplied to the muscles at a faster rate during exercise.   *(2 marks)*

ii Name **one** waste substance that must be removed from the muscles at a faster rate during exercise.   *(1 mark)*

Study tip

Question 2 has a graph and calculations. Some students lose marks by not reading the axes of the graph carefully. Always double check your readings and remember that for 2b you must multiply by 4 to get beats per minute. If you use a calculator, make sure you tap in the correct numbers. Students often lose marks because they assume the calculator is always correct.

3 Gardeners buy packets of dry seeds. Before planting, the dry seeds must be soaked in water. When the soaked seeds are planted they will germinate (sprout) and eventually grow into plants.

Some students wanted to investigate the process of respiration in pea seeds. The students predicted that some of the energy released in respiration will heat the surroundings.

One group of students set up two thermos flasks as shown in Diagram 1.

a The students used thermometers with a temperature range of 0°C to 100°C. They decided to record the temperature every 6 hours.

   i The readings are likely to be inaccurate. Explain why.
   (2 marks)

   ii Suggest how to monitor the temperature more accurately.
   (2 marks)

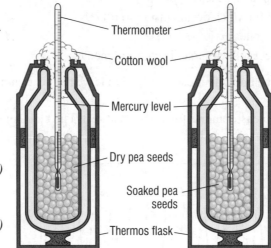

Diagram 1

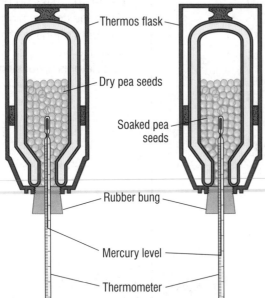

Diagram 2

b A second group of students decided to turn the flasks upside down and hold them in a clamp. To stop the thermometers falling out they used rubber bungs with a hole for the thermometer. They set up the flasks as shown in Diagram 2.

   i What is the advantage of inverting the flasks? *(2 marks)*

   ii What is the disadvantage of using rubber bungs instead of cotton wool? *(1 mark)*

c A third group of students decided it would be an improvement to use **boiled**, soaked peas as a control. After four days they noticed that the temperature in the control flask was higher than in the experimental flask with soaked peas which had not been boiled.

   i Explain the reason for this result. *(3 marks)*

   ii How could the third group improve the design of their experiment? *(2 marks)*

B7.1 Principles of homeostasis

Key points

- Homeostasis is the process by which automatic control systems, including your nervous system, your hormones and your body organs, maintain almost constant conditions.
- Homeostasis is important because the body cells need almost constant conditions to work properly.
- Humans need to maintain a constant internal environment, controlling levels of water, ions and blood glucose as well as temperature.

The process by which your body maintains a constant **internal environment** is called **homeostasis**.

Homeostasis relies on automatic control systems such as your nervous system, **hormones** and your body organs.

Internal conditions that are controlled include:

- water content
- ion content
- temperature
- blood sugar level.

Water is leaving the body all the time as we breathe out and sweat. We lose any excess water in the urine (produced by the **kidneys**). We also lose ions in our sweat and in the urine.

We must keep our **core body temperature** constant, otherwise the enzymes in the body will not work properly (or may not work at all). If we get too cold, we suffer from **hypothermia** and our cells stop working.

1 *Why is it important to control our body temperature?*

Sugar in the blood is the energy source for cells. The level of sugar in our blood is controlled by the pancreas.

2 *Which organ controls blood sugar levels?*

links

Revise more on the nervous system, including control systems and receptors, in 6.1 'Responding to change and receptors'. Revise more on osmosis in 1.5 'Osmosis'.

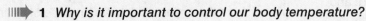

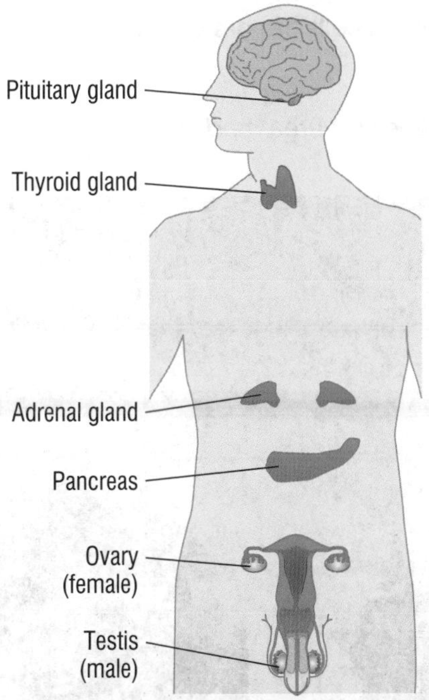

Pituitary gland

Thyroid gland

Adrenal gland

Pancreas

Ovary (female)

Testis (male)

Figure 1 Hormones act as chemical messages. They are made in glands in one part of the body, but have an effect somewhere else.

Study tip

Sweating affects both temperature AND water content of the body. It cools the body by using heat energy from the skin to evaporate the water.

Key words: internal environment, homeostasis, hormone, kidney, core body temperature, hypothermia

Study tip

To improve your grade make sure you understand why internal conditions should be kept within very small limits. Link the condition to the reason why it must be kept constant.

Student Book
pages 82–83

B7.2 Removing waste products

The internal conditions of the body must be carefully controlled. Your body cells are constantly producing waste substances that must be removed.

Waste products that have to be removed from the body include:
- carbon dioxide, produced by respiration, removed via the lungs when we breathe out
- urea, produced in the **liver** from the breakdown of amino acids, removed by the kidneys in the urine and temporarily stored in the bladder
- water and ions which enter the body when we eat and drink. If the water or ion content in the body is wrong, too much water may move into or out of the cells. This could damage or destroy the cells.

1 Where is carbon dioxide made?

The liver

The liver is a large organ that has many different functions and is very important in homeostasis.

- Excess amino acids are changed to urea in the liver. The amino group is removed from the amino acid in the process of deamination. This forms ammonia, a toxic substance, which is then converted to urea. The urea passes in the blood to the kidneys and is excreted (removed) in the urine.

$$\text{amino acids} \xrightarrow{\text{deamination in liver}} \text{ammonia} \to \text{urea} \xrightarrow{\text{in blood to kidneys}} \text{urine}$$

- Poisonous substances such as ethanol are detoxified, and the breakdown products excreted in the urine.
- Old red blood cells are broken down and the iron is stored to make new red blood cells.

2 Where is urea made?

Key points

- Carbon dioxide is produced during respiration and leaves the body via the lungs when you breathe out.
- Urea is produced by your liver as excess amino acids are broken down, and is removed by your kidneys in the urine.

Study tip

Don't confuse *urea* and *urine*. Urea is a waste molecule made in the liver, carried to the kidneys in the blood, and excreted in the urine.

∞ links

Revise more on the removal of carbon dioxide from the body in 4.1 'Breathing and gas exchange in the lungs'.
Revise more on osmosis in 1.5 'Osmosis', body temperature in 7.6 'Controlling body temperature' and controlling glucose levels in 7.7 'Controlling blood glucose'.

Key word: liver

Figure 1 The internal conditions of the human body hardly vary despite our surroundings

Student Book
pages 84–85

B7.3 The human kidney

The kidneys

The body has two kidneys. They **filter** the blood, excreting substances you do not want and keeping those substances that the body needs.

A healthy kidney produces urine by:
- first filtering the blood
- reabsorbing all the sugar
- reabsorbing the dissolved ions needed by the body
- reabsorbing as much water as the body needs
- releasing urea, excess ions and water in the urine.

As all the sugar and only some water, ions and urea are reabsorbed, we call this **selective reabsorption**.

The urine is temporarily stored in the **bladder** before being removed from the body.

▐▐▐▶ **1** *What two processes occur in the kidney to make urine?*

ADH and the water balance of your blood

- If the water content of the blood is too low, the pituitary gland releases a hormone called **ADH** into the blood. This causes the kidneys to reabsorb more water and results in more concentrated urine.
- If the water content of the blood is too high, less ADH is released into the blood. Less water is reabsorbed in the kidneys, resulting in more dilute urine.
- Keeping the water balance is a **negative feedback system**. As the water level in the blood rises, it stops the production of more ADH.

▐▐▐▶ **2** *What is ADH and where is it produced?*

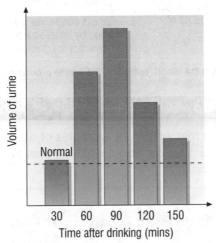 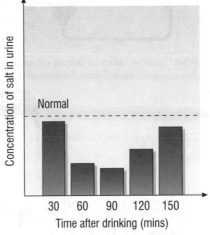

Figure 1 These data show how your kidneys respond when you drink a lot. They show the volume of urine produced and the concentration of salt in the urine after a student drank a large volume of water.

Key words: selective reabsorption, bladder, ADH, negative feedback system

Key points

- The kidneys are important for excretion and homeostasis.
- A healthy kidney produces urine by filtering the blood. It then reabsorbs all of the glucose, plus any mineral ions and water needed by your body.
- Excess mineral ions and water, along with urea, are removed in the urine.
- The water balance of the blood is maintained by the hormone ADH, which changes the amount of water reabsorbed by the kidney.

◯◯ links

Revise more on the movement of molecules and ions across partially permeable membranes in 1.4 'Diffusion' and in 1.6 'Active transport'.

Study tip

Understand that *all* small molecules are filtered in the kidney, but the useful ones such as glucose are reabsorbed. Only large molecules such as proteins cannot be filtered.

Student Book
pages 86–87

B7.4 Dialysis – an artificial kidney

Key points

- People suffering from kidney failure may be treated by regular sessions on a kidney dialysis machine or by having a kidney transplant.
- In a dialysis machine, the concentration of dissolved substances in the blood is restored to normal levels.
- The levels of useful substances in the blood are maintained, while urea and excess mineral ions pass out from the blood into the dialysis fluid.

- If a person suffers from kidney failure, they can be kept alive by **dialysis**.
- A **dialysis machine** carries out the same job as the kidneys. The blood flows between partially permeable membranes.
- The dialysis fluid contains the same concentration of useful substances as the patient's blood, e.g. glucose and mineral ions. This means that these substances do not diffuse out of the blood, so they do not need to be reabsorbed. Urea diffuses out from the blood into the dialysis fluid.
- Dialysis restores the concentration of substances in the blood back to normal, but needs to be carried out at regular intervals.

> 1 What is the purpose of dialysis?

- If a kidney becomes available, the patient may have a **kidney transplant**. If the transplant is successful, the person will not need further dialysis.

> 2 What is the alternative treatment to dialysis?

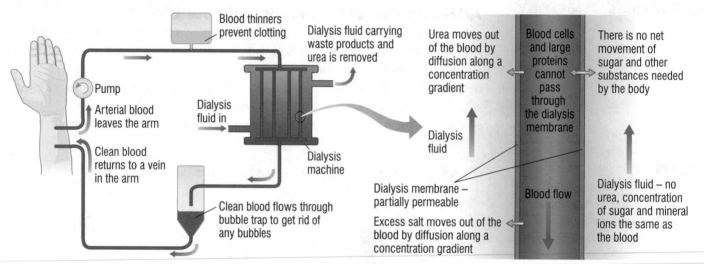

Figure 1 A dialysis machine relies on simple diffusion to clean the blood, removing the waste products that would damage the body as they build up

links
Revise more on diffusion in 1.4 'Diffusion'.

Study tip
Look at as many different examples of dialysis diagrams as you can. Identify the membrane. Be clear about what diffuses through the membrane. What is in the dialysis fluid?

Key words: dialysis, dialysis machine, kidney transplant

Student Book
pages 88–89

B7.5 Kidney transplants

Key points

- In a kidney transplant, a healthy kidney from a donor replaces the function of the diseased or damaged kidney.
- To try and prevent rejection of the donor kidney, the tissue types of the donor and the recipient are matched as closely as possible. Immunosuppressant drugs are also used.

- For most patients a kidney transplant is a better option than dialysis. The diseased kidney is replaced with a healthy one.
- Kidneys may be obtained from a victim of a fatal accident or sometimes from living donors, as a person only needs one kidney to live a normal life.
- The new kidney must be a very good 'tissue match' to prevent rejection.
- There are proteins called antigens on the surface of cells. The recipient's antibodies may attack the antigens on the donor organ because they recognise them as being 'foreign'.
- Following the transplant, the recipient must take drugs to suppress the **immune response** to prevent rejection. These are called immunosuppressant drugs.

1 *What are antigens?*

- Despite the advantages of a transplant, there are some risks from operations. Treatment before and following the transplant involves suppressing the patient's immune system, which leaves them vulnerable to common infections.

2 *What is the main advantage of a kidney transplant compared with dialysis?*

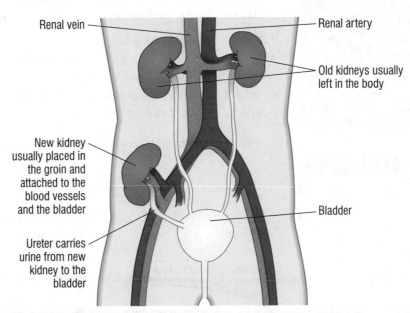

Renal vein

Renal artery

Old kidneys usually left in the body

New kidney usually placed in the groin and attached to the blood vessels and the bladder

Bladder

Ureter carries urine from new kidney to the bladder

Figure 1 A donor kidney takes over the functions of failed kidneys, which are usually left in place

⬭ links

Revise more on antigens in 8.3 'Immunity' and on stem cell research in 2.3 'Stem cells'.

Study tip

When evaluating advantages/disadvantages of transplants in an exam, use your own knowledge and select information carefully from the introduction to the question to give a balanced argument. Always write a conclusion backed up by the evidence.

Key word: immune response

Student Book
pages 90–91

B7.6

Controlling body temperature

Key points

- Your body temperature is monitored and controlled by the thermoregulatory centre in your brain.

- Your body responds to cool you down or warm you up if your core body temperature changes, so it is maintained at around 37 °C.

- The blood vessels that supply the capillaries in the skin dilate and constrict to control the blood flow to the surface capillaries.

- Heat energy is released through the evaporation of water in sweat from the surface of the skin to cool the body down.

- Shivering involves contraction of the muscles that releases energy from respiration to warm the body.

Study tip

Never say that capillaries dilate or constrict. They are not able to do this as they have no muscle cells! Instead, it is the blood vessels supplying the capillaries that dilate or constrict.

Also blood vessels *never* move! Either more blood flows in vessels near the skin surface, or more blood flows in the vessels lower down.

∞ links

Revise more on enzyme reactions in 3.3 'Factors affecting enzyme action'.

Human body temperature must be kept at about 37 °C so that the enzymes will work efficiently. The **core body temperature**, deep inside the body, must be kept stable.

- Body temperature is monitored and controlled by the **thermoregulatory centre** in the brain. This centre has receptors which detect the temperature of the blood flowing through the brain.

- Temperature receptors in the skin also send impulses to the brain to give information about skin temperature.

- The skin looks red when we are hot due to increased blood flow.

- Sweating helps to cool the body. When it is hot, more water is lost from the skin so more water must be taken in with drinks and food to balance this loss.

|||➡ **1** *Where is blood temperature monitored?*

If the core temperature *rises*:

- blood vessels near the surface of the skin dilate, allowing more blood to flow through the skin capillaries. Energy is transferred by radiation and the skin cools.

- sweat glands produce more sweat. The water in sweat evaporates from the skin's surface. The energy required for the water to evaporate comes from the skin's surface. So we cool down.

If the core temperature *falls*:

- blood vessels near the surface of the skin constrict and less blood flows through the skin capillaries. Less energy is radiated.

- we 'shiver'. Muscles contract quickly. This requires respiration, and some of the energy released warms the blood.

|||➡ **2** *Explain why sweating cools the body.*

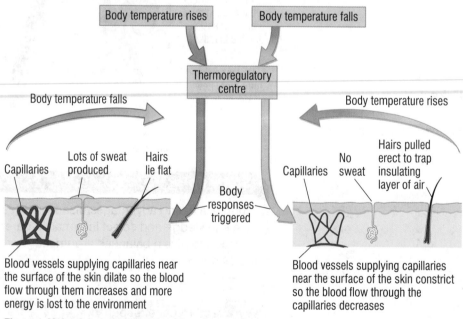

Figure 1 Maintaining a steady internal environment

Key word: thermoregulatory centre

B7.7 Controlling blood glucose

The pancreas monitors and controls the level of glucose in our blood. Receptors in the pancreas detect the level of blood glucose.

High levels of blood glucose
- If there is too much glucose in our blood, the pancreas produces the hormone **insulin**.
- Insulin causes the glucose to move from the blood into the cells.
- In the liver and muscles, excess glucose is converted to **glycogen** for storage. When these stores are full, the glucose is stored as lipid and this can eventually make a person **obese**.

▥▶ **1 Which hormone reduces the level of glucose in the blood?**

Low levels of blood glucose
- Insulin causes the blood glucose level to fall.
- If the level gets too low, receptors in the pancreas detect the low level.
- The pancreas releases **glucagon**, another hormone.
- The glucagon causes the glycogen in the liver to change into glucose.
- This glucose is released back into the blood.

▥▶ **2 Which hormone causes blood sugar to rise?**

Diabetes
- If no, or too little, insulin is produced by the pancreas, the blood glucose level may become very high. This condition is known as **type 1 diabetes**.
- Type 1 diabetes is controlled by injections of insulin and careful attention to diet and levels of exercise.
- **Type 2 diabetes** develops when the body does not respond to its own insulin. Obesity is a significant factor in the development of type 2 diabetes.
- Type 2 diabetes can be controlled by careful diet, exercise and by drugs that help the cells to respond to insulin.

Key points

- Your blood glucose concentration is monitored and controlled by your pancreas.
- The pancreas produces the hormone insulin, which allows glucose to move from the blood into the cells and to be stored as glycogen in the liver and muscles.
- The pancreas also produces glucagon, which allows glycogen to be converted back into glucose and released into the blood.
- In type 1 diabetes, the blood glucose may rise to fatally high levels because the pancreas does not secrete enough insulin.
- In type 2 diabetes, the body stops responding to its own insulin.

Study tip

Make sure you know the difference between:
- glucose – the sugar used in respiration
- glycogen – a storage carbohydrate found in the liver and muscles
- glucagon – a hormone.

If you cannot spell these words correctly, you are likely to lose marks in the exam.

Key words: insulin, obese, glucagon, type 1 diabetes, type 2 diabetes

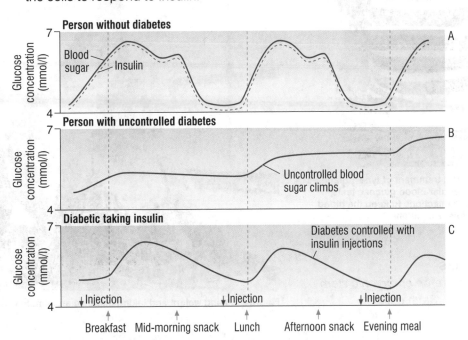

Figure 1 These graphs show the impact insulin injections have on people with type 1 diabetes. The injections keep the blood glucose level within safe limits.

Treating diabetes

- In the past, there was no effective treatment for diabetes and people with the condition eventually died.
- Today, type 1 diabetes may be controlled by injecting insulin, careful diet control and exercise.
- Type 2 diabetes is often treated by careful attention to diet and taking more exercise. If this doesn't work, drugs may be needed.
- Currently, a variety of different methods are being used or developed to treat diabetes using genetic engineering and stem cell techniques.

- Type 1 diabetes is traditionally treated with human insulin produced by genetically engineered bacteria.
- The person with type 1 diabetes has to inject before meals every day of their life.
- Very active diabetics have to match the amount of insulin injected with their diet and exercise.
- Some diabetics use pumps attached to the body. They can adjust the level of insulin injected by the pump.

Doctors and other scientists are trying to develop new methods of treating and possibly curing type 1 diabetes. These include:

- pancreas transplants
- transplanting pancreas cells
- using embryonic stem cells to produce insulin-secreting cells
- using adult stem cells from diabetic patients
- genetically engineering pancreas cells to make them work properly.

 1 *Name two new methods that are being developed to treat type 1 diabetes.*

If controlling your diet, losing weight and exercise do not work, doctors can prescribe drugs to treat type 2 diabetes. The drugs help:

- insulin to work better
- the pancreas to make more insulin
- to reduce the amount of glucose you absorb from your gut.

2 *How do drugs help in type 2 diabetes? Give one reason.*

Figure 1 The treatment of type 1 diabetes involves regular blood glucose tests and insulin injections to keep the blood glucose levels constant

⦾ links

Revise more on embryonic stem cells in 2.3 'Stem cells'.

Figure 2 Losing weight and taking exercise are simple ways to help overcome type 2 diabetes

1 How is urea made?

2 Which process in the body produces carbon dioxide?

3 What is meant by 'homeostasis'?

4 Give two functions of the liver.

5 Where are the receptors that detect both blood temperature and water content?

6 How does the pancreas detect blood glucose levels?

7 Glucose and mineral ions can be reabsorbed by the kidney against a concentration gradient. What process can make this happen?

8 What is the difference between glucagon and glycogen?

9 Describe what happens to control the level of water in the blood if a person drinks a large volume of water.

10 How can a person help to prevent themselves from developing type 2 diabetes?

11 Why does a dialysis machine contain a solution rather than water?

Study tip

Before evaluating the information about new methods of treating type 1 diabetes, read all of the data very carefully. Marks are often lost when students only try to remember ideas they have been taught and do not refer to the introduction to the question.

Chapter checklist

Tick when you have:

	✓		
reviewed it after your lesson	✓		
revised once – some questions right	✓	✓	
revised twice – all questions right	✓	✓	✓

Move on to another topic when you have all three ticks

Principles of homeostasis	☐	☐	☐
Removing waste products	☐	☐	☐
The human kidney	☐	☐	☐
Dialysis – an artificial kidney	☐	☐	☐
Kidney transplants	☐	☐	☐
Controlling body temperature	☐	☐	☐
Controlling blood glucose	☐	☐	☐
Treating diabetes	☐	☐	☐

Student Book
pages 98–99

B8.1

Pathogens and disease

Key points

- Infectious diseases are caused by microorganisms called pathogens, such as bacteria and viruses.
- Bacteria and viruses reproduce rapidly inside your body. Bacteria can produce toxins that make you feel ill.
- Viruses damage your cells as they reproduce. This can also make you feel ill.

- **Pathogens** cause **infectious diseases**.
- Pathogens are tiny **microorganisms** – usually bacteria or viruses.
- When bacteria or **viruses** enter the body they reproduce rapidly. They can make you feel ill by producing toxins (poisons).
- Viruses are much smaller than bacteria and reproduce inside cells. The damage to the cells also makes you ill.

▶ **1** *How do pathogens make you feel ill?*

- Before bacteria and viruses had been discovered, a doctor called Semmelweis realised that infection could be transferred from person to person in a hospital – infected people are said to be **infectious**.
- Semmelweis told his staff to wash their hands between treating patients. However, other doctors did not take him seriously. We now know that he was right!

▶ **2** *Why did it take a long time for others to accept the ideas of Semmelweis?*

links
Revise more on bacteria that are resistant to antibiotics in 8.5 'Changing pathogens'.

Key words: pathogen, infectious disease, microorganism, virus, infectious

Student Book
pages 100–101

B8.2

Defence mechanisms

Key points

- Your body has several methods of defending itself against the entry of pathogens. These include the skin, the mucus of the breathing system and the clotting of the blood.
- Your white blood cells help to defend you against pathogens by ingesting them, making antibodies and making antitoxins.

- Pathogens can be transmitted from one person to another by **droplet infection** or **direct contact**. When you cough or sneeze pathogens are sprayed into the air in drops of water.
- The skin prevents pathogens getting into the body.
- Pathogens are also trapped by mucus and killed by stomach acid.

▶ **1** *How are many pathogens prevented from entering the body?*

White blood cells are part of the immune system. They do three things to defend the body:

- They can ingest pathogens. This means they digest and destroy them.
- They produce antibodies to help destroy particular pathogens.
- They produce antitoxins to counteract the toxins (poisons) that pathogens produce.

▶ **2** *How do white blood cells defend the body?*

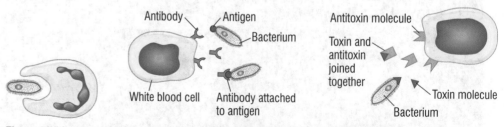

Figure 1 White blood cells ingest bacteria, make antibodies and make antitoxins

links
Revise more on blood and clotting in 5.4 'Transport in the blood'.

Key words: droplet infection, direct contact

B8.3 Immunity

Key points

- The white blood cells of your immune system produce antibodies to destroy particular pathogens. Your body will then respond rapidly to future infections by the same pathogen by making the correct antibody very rapidly. In this way, you become immune to the disease.

- You can be immunised against a disease by introducing small amounts of dead or inactive pathogens into your body.

- We can use vaccinations to protect against both bacterial and viral pathogens.

- Dead or inactive forms of a pathogen are used to make a **vaccine**. Vaccines can be injected into the body.
- The white blood cells react by producing antibodies.
- This makes the person immune. It prevents further infection because the body responds quickly by producing more antibodies.
- The antibodies recognise the antigen (the protein shape) on the pathogen.
- The MMR **vaccination** (**immunisation**) is one of several vaccines. MMR is given to prevent measles, mumps and rubella.
- Most people in a population need to be vaccinated to protect society from very serious diseases. This is known as **herd immunity**.

1 *What is meant by 'vaccination'?*

2 *How do antibodies 'recognise' antigens?*

Study tip

High levels of antibodies do not stay in your blood forever – immunity is the ability of your white blood cells to produce the right antibodies quickly, if you are reinfected.

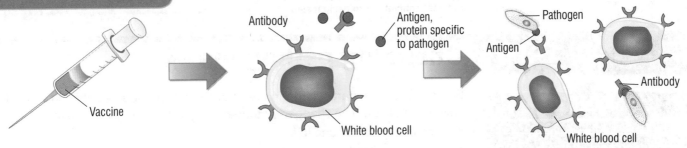

Small amounts of dead or inactive pathogen are put into your body, often by injection.

The antigens in the vaccine stimulate your white blood cells into making antibodies. The antibodies destroy the antigens without any risk of you getting the disease.

You are immune to future infections by the pathogen. That's because your body can respond rapidly and make the correct antibody as if you had already had the disease.

Figure 1 This is how vaccines protect you against dangerous infectious diseases

Key words: vaccine, vaccination, immunisation, herd immunity

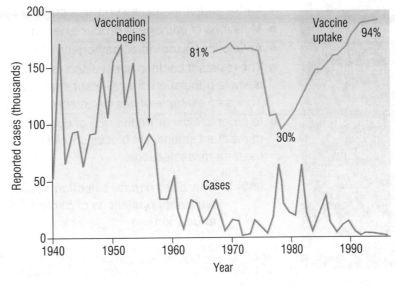

Figure 2 Graph showing the effect of the whooping cough scare on both uptake of the vaccine and the number of cases of the disease (Source: Open University)

B8.4 Using drugs to treat disease

Key points

- Some medicines relieve the symptoms of disease but do not kill the pathogens which cause it.
- Antibiotics cure bacterial diseases by killing the bacteria inside your body.
- Antibiotics do not destroy viruses because the viruses reproduce inside the cells. It is difficult to develop drugs that can destroy viruses without damaging your body cells.

Key word: drug

- Antibiotics kill infective bacteria in the body.
- Penicillin is an antibiotic, but there are many others. It was first discovered by Alexander Fleming in 1928.
- Viruses are difficult to kill because they reproduce inside the body cells, so any treatment could also damage the body cells.
- Painkillers and other **drugs** relieve the symptoms of a disease, but do not kill the pathogen.
- Your immune system will usually overcome the viral pathogens.

▶ **1** *Why are antibiotics only able to kill bacteria?*

Figure 1 Penicillin was the first antibiotic. Now we have many different ones which kill different types of bacterium. Here, several different antibiotics are being tested.

Study tip

Don't confuse antiseptic, antibodies and antibiotics.
- Antiseptic is a liquid which kills microorganisms in the environment.
- Antibiotics are drugs that kill bacteria (NOT viruses) in the body.
- Antibodies are proteins made by white blood cells to kill pathogens (both bacteria AND viruses).

B8.5 Changing pathogens

Key points

- Mutations of pathogens produce new strains.
- Antibiotics kill the non-resistant strain of bacteria, but individual resistant pathogens survive and reproduce, so the population of the resistant strain increases by natural selection.
- Existing antibiotics and vaccines may not be effective against the new resistant strain.
- To prevent the problem getting worse, it is important not to overuse antibiotics, to use the correct antibiotics and to complete each course of medicine.
- The development of antibiotic resistance means new antibiotics must be developed.

Some pathogens, particularly viruses, can mutate (change) resulting in a new form called a mutation. The changed pathogen can spread rapidly because:

- people are not immune to it
- there is no effective treatment.

▶ **1** *Why do some pathogens spread rapidly?*

Antibiotic-resistant bacteria

- The **MRSA** 'super bug' is a bacterium that has evolved through **natural selection**. MRSA and other bacteria have become resistant to the common antibiotics.
- Mutations of pathogens produce new strains, some are resistant to antibiotics.
- Antibiotics kill individual pathogens of the non-resistant strain.
- The resistant bacteria survive and reproduce and a whole population of a resistant strain develops. This is an example of natural selection.
- In order to slow down the rate of development of resistant strains, antibiotics should not be used for mild infections.

▶ **2** *How does natural selection cause resistant populations of bacteria to develop?*

Key words: MRSA, natural selection

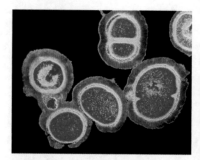

Figure 1 MRSA bacteria (the bacterium methicillin-resistant *Staphylococcus aureus*) magnified 9560 times by a scanning electron microscope

Growing and investigating bacteria

Key points

- An uncontaminated culture of microorganisms can be grown using sterilised Petri dishes and agar. You sterilise the inoculating loop before use and fix the lid of the Petri dish to prevent unwanted microorganisms getting in. The culture is left upside down at about 25°C for a few days.

- Uncontaminated cultures are needed so we can investigate the effect of chemicals such as disinfectants and antibiotics on microorganisms.

- Cultures should be incubated at a maximum temperature of 25°C in schools and colleges to reduce the likelihood of harmful pathogens growing, although in industry they are cultured at higher temperatures.

- Pure cultures of non-pathogenic (safe) bacteria can be used for laboratory investigations.
- A culture of microorganisms can be used to find the effect of antibiotics on bacteria.
- Investigations need uncontaminated cultures of microorganisms. Strict health and safety procedures are used to protect yourself and others.
- Contamination might come from your skin, the air, the soil or the water around you.
- If the culture is contaminated, other bacteria could grow, including pathogens.

Growing cultures

To culture (grow) microorganisms in a laboratory you must:
- give them a liquid or gel containing nutrients – a **culture medium**. It contains carbohydrate as an energy source, various minerals and sometimes other chemicals. A culture medium called **agar** jelly is used.
- provide warmth and oxygen
- keep them incubated at 25°C in school laboratories and at 35°C in industry.

> **1** *Why do industrial laboratories use 35°C instead of 25°C as in schools?*

To keep the culture pure you must:
- kill all the bacteria on the equipment – pass metal loops through a flame; boil solutions and agar
- use the sterilised metal loop to transfer the culture to **inoculate** the sterile agar
- prevent microorganisms from the air getting into the equipment
- prevent microorganisms leaving the Petri dish in case there has been a **mutation**.

> **2** *How do you make sure that unwanted microorganisms do not contaminate a pure culture of bacteria?*

Place the inoculating loop in a flame to sterilise it. Let it cool.

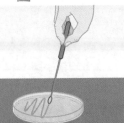

Dip the sterilised loop in a suspension of the bacteria and make zigzag streaks across the surface of the agar.

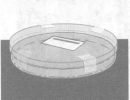

Replace the lid quickly and tape as shown. This avoids contamination and allows oxygen in to prevent growth of harmful anaerobic bacteria.

Figure 1 Culturing microorganisms safely in the laboratory

Practical

Investigating the effectiveness of disinfectants and antibiotics

Investigate the effect of disinfectants and antibiotics on the growth of bacteria by adding circles of filter paper soaked in different types or concentrations of disinfectant or antibiotic when you set up your culture plate.

> **3** *Look at the plate. How do you know if the bacteria have been killed by the antibiotic?*

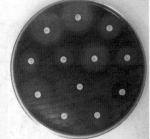

Figure 2 Culturing microorganisms makes it possible for us to observe how different chemicals affect them

Key words: culture medium, agar, inoculate, mutation

1 What is a pathogen?

2 List four ways you can protect yourself or others against infection.

3 Why is it difficult to produce medicines to destroy viruses?

4 What changes in a pathogen when it mutates?

5 Some mutated pathogens are dangerous. Why?

6 What is the difference between an antibiotic and an antiseptic?

7 What is meant by a 'pure culture' of bacteria?

8 Why do we do the following when transferring a pure culture from a bottle to agar jelly in a Petri dish?

a Pass a metal loop through a flame.

b Cool the loop before placing in the culture.

c Hold the lid of the dish at an angle when streaking the agar jelly.

d Incubate at not more than 25 °C.

9 Explain how bacteria develop antibiotic resistance.

10 What is contained in a vaccine?

11 Explain how a person develops immunity following vaccination.

Study tip

Remember there are three ways in which white blood cells defend the body.

Chapter checklist ✓ ✓ ✓

Tick when you have:

reviewed it after your lesson ✓ ☐ ☐

revised once – some questions right ✓ ✓ ☐

revised twice – all questions right ✓ ✓ ✓

Move on to another topic when you have all three ticks

Pathogens and disease	☐ ☐ ☐
Defence mechanisms	☐ ☐ ☐
Immunity	☐ ☐ ☐
Using drugs to treat disease	☐ ☐ ☐
Changing pathogens	☐ ☐ ☐
Growing and investigating bacteria	☐ ☐ ☐

B9.1 Photosynthesis

Key points

- During photosynthesis, light energy is absorbed by chlorophyll in the chloroplasts of the green parts of the plant. It is used to convert carbon dioxide and water into sugar (glucose). Oxygen is released as a by-product.

- Photosynthesis can be summed up by the following word and balanced symbol equation:

  carbon dioxide + water $\xrightarrow{\text{light energy}}$ glucose + oxygen

  $6CO_2$ + $6H_2O$ $\xrightarrow{\text{light energy}}$ $C_6H_{12}O_6$ + $6O_2$

- Leaves are well adapted to allow the maximum amount of photosynthesis to take place.

Study tip

Practise labelling the parts and cells in the cross-section of a leaf, and be sure you know the function of each one.

⊙⊙ links

Revise more on the structure and function of plant cells in 1.1 'Animal and plant cells'.

Figure 2 The oxygen produced during photosynthesis is vital for life on Earth. You can demonstrate that it is produced using water plants such as this *Cabomba*.

Photosynthesis can only be carried out by green plants and algae.

- Chlorophyll in the chloroplasts absorbs the Sun's light energy.
- The equation for photosynthesis is:

  carbon dioxide + water $\xrightarrow{\text{light energy}}$ glucose + oxygen

  $6CO_2$ + $6H_2O$ $\xrightarrow{\text{light energy}}$ $C_6H_{12}O_6$ + $6O_2$

- The process for photosynthesis is:
  1 Carbon dioxide is taken in by the leaves, and water is taken up by the roots.
  2 The chlorophyll traps the light energy needed for photosynthesis.
  3 This energy is used to convert the carbon dioxide and water into **glucose** (a sugar).
- Oxygen is released as a by-product of photosynthesis.
- Some of the glucose is converted into insoluble starch for storage.

▐▐▶ 1 *Where does the energy for photosynthesis come from?*

Practical

Testing a leaf for starch

By testing leaves with iodine solution (the **iodine test** for starch) we can identify the starch in the leaf and show that photosynthesis has occurred. Variegated leaves have patches of green (with chlorophyll) and white (without chlorophyll). Only the green patches will turn the iodine solution blue-black to show that starch has been made.

▐▐▶ 2 *What colour will the iodine solution stain the leaf after it has been placed in the dark for 48 hours? Explain your answer.*

Figure 1 These variegated leaves came from a plant which had been kept in the light for several hours. The one on the right has been tested for starch, using iodine solution.

Practical

Producing oxygen

When a plant photosynthesises it gives off oxygen. Bubbles of oxygen can be collected when a water plant is exposed to light.

▐▐▶ 3 *Why are water plants used in this experiment?*

Key word: glucose

Limiting factors

Key points

- The rate of photosynthesis may be limited by shortage of light, low temperature and shortage of carbon dioxide.
- We can artificially control levels of light, temperature and carbon dioxide when growing crops in greenhouses to increase the rate of photosynthesis and so increase the yield of the crops.

Key words: limiting factor, polytunnel

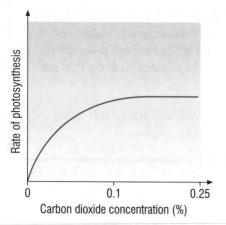

Figure 1 The effect of increasing carbon dioxide levels on the rate of photosynthesis at a particular light level and temperature. Eventually one of the other factors becomes limiting.

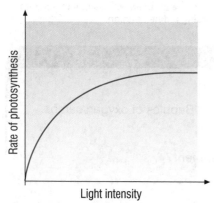

Figure 2 The effect of light intensity on the rate of photosynthesis

- A lack of light would slow down the rate of photosynthesis as light provides the energy for the process. Even on sunny days, light may be limited to plants which are shaded by trees.
- If it is cold, then enzymes do not work effectively and this will slow down the rate of photosynthesis.
- If there is too little carbon dioxide, then the rate of photosynthesis will slow down. Carbon dioxide may be limited in an enclosed space, e.g. in a greenhouse on a sunny day where there is plenty of light energy available but the plants run out of carbon dioxide.

▶ **1** *Why does photosynthesis slow down in cold conditions?*

- Anything that stops the rate of photosynthesis increasing above a certain level is a **limiting factor**.
- It is difficult to control limiting factors in fields where crops are growing. Farmers use greenhouses and **polytunnels** to increase the yields of their crops. The conditions are varied to ensure that plants photosynthesise for as long as possible:
  - the temperature is maintained at the optimum for enzyme action
  - carbon dioxide levels are increased so they do not become a limiting factor
  - artificial lighting can be used to extend the hours, and the months, when plants photosynthesise.
- Using greenhouses can be costly in terms of buildings, electricity (used for heating and lighting) and control systems such as computers. However, higher yields mean more profits.

Study tip

Make sure you can explain why a factor is limiting. The most difficult questions involve interpretation of graphs. Always check the axes of the graph to work out which are the independent and the dependent variables.

Practical

Planning photosynthesis experiments

When carrying out photosynthesis experiments you need to know which factor is being changed and which factors must be controlled. If you want to find out the effect of increasing carbon dioxide levels, then you must be aware that other factors such as light may limit the rate of photosynthesis.

The **independent variable** is the one being tested, e.g. concentration of carbon dioxide.

The **dependent variable** is the one you measure to judge the effect of changing the independent variable – in this case it is usually the volume of oxygen produced.

Variables which need to be controlled are light, temperature and the type of plant being used.

▶ **2** *Which gas do you collect to show that a plant is photosynthesising?*

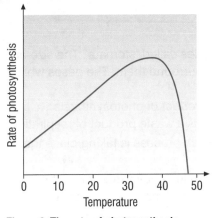

Rate of photosynthesis (y-axis)
Temperature (x-axis): 0 10 20 30 40 50

Figure 3 The rate of photosynthesis increases steadily with a rise in temperature up to a certain point. After this the enzymes are destroyed and the reaction stops completely.

Figure 4 By controlling the temperature, light and carbon dioxide levels in a greenhouse like this you can produce the biggest possible crops – fast!

Student Book pages 116–117	**B9.3**

How plants use glucose

The uses of soluble glucose

- The glucose produced by photosynthesis may be:
  – converted into insoluble starch for storage in organs such as a potato **tuber**
  – used for respiration
  – converted into fats and oils for storage
  – used to produce cellulose which strengthens cell walls
  – used to produce proteins.
- Plant and algal cells also need a supply of **mineral ions** such as **nitrate ions** in order to produce protein. Plants absorb nitrate ions from the soil. Algae absorb nitrate ions from the water they live in.

> **1** *Name three substances used for storage in plants.*

- Carnivorous plants such as the Venus flytrap are adapted to live in nutrient-poor soil.
- The Venus flytrap obtains most of its nutrients from the animals, such as insects, that it catches and digests. The plant obtains nitrates by digesting animal protein.

> **2** *What is meant by the term 'carnivorous plant'?*

Study tip

Two important points to remember:
- Plants respire 24 hours a day to release energy.
- Glucose is soluble in water, but starch is insoluble.

◯◯ links

Revise more on transport in plants in 9.6 'Transport systems in plants' and osmosis in plants in 1.5 'Osmosis'.

Key words: tuber, mineral ion, nitrate ion

Key points

- Plant and algal cells use the soluble glucose they produce during photosynthesis for respiration, to convert into insoluble starch for storage, to produce fats or oils for storage, and to produce fats, proteins or cellulose for use in the cells and cell walls.
- Plant and algal cells also need other materials including nitrate ions to make the amino acids which make up proteins.
- Carnivorous plants are adapted to live in nutrient-poor soil by taking minerals from the animals they catch and digest.

Figure 1 The Venus flytrap – an insect-eating plant

B9.4 Exchange in plants

- Gases diffuse in and out of leaves through tiny holes called 'stomata'. The size of the stomata is controlled by the **guard cells** that surround them. The gases which diffuse through stomata are:
  – oxygen: needed for respiration and is a waste product of photosynthesis
  – carbon dioxide: needed for photosynthesis and is a waste product of respiration.
- The movement of these gases depends upon which process is taking place the most quickly.
- Plants also lose water vapour through the stomata due to **evaporation** in the leaves. The water cannot diffuse through the surface of the leaf because it is covered by a waxy **cuticle**.

▐▐▐▶ **1 Why do leaves have stomata?**

- Leaves are flat and very thin so the gases do not need to diffuse very far. There are also internal air spaces.
- Water and mineral ions are taken up by the roots. **Root hair cells** increase the surface area of roots for the absorption of water and mineral ions.
- If plants lose water faster than it is replaced by the roots, the stomata can close to prevent wilting.

▐▐▐▶ **2 How do plants prevent wilting?**

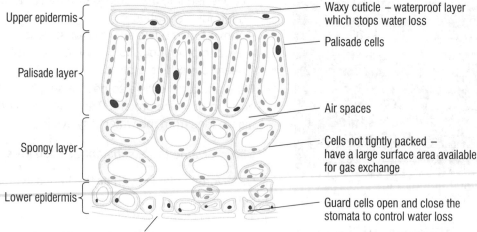

Upper epidermis — Waxy cuticle – waterproof layer which stops water loss

Palisade layer — Palisade cells

Spongy layer — Air spaces

Cells not tightly packed – have a large surface area available for gas exchange

Lower epidermis — Guard cells open and close the stomata to control water loss

Stomata like this allow gases to move in and out of the leaf

Figure 1 This is a cross-section of a leaf showing the arrangement of the cells inside, with plenty of air spaces and short diffusion distances. This means that the carbon dioxide needed for photosynthesis reaches the cells as efficiently as possible.

Key words: guard cell, evaporation, cuticle, root hair cell

Student Book
pages 120–121

B9.5 Evaporation and transpiration

- Plants take up water through the roots. The water passes through the plant to the leaves. In the leaves the water evaporates from the leaf cells and the water vapour diffuses out through the stomata – this is known as **transpiration**.
- The movement of the water through the plant is called the **transpiration stream**.
- The plant could dehydrate if the rate of evaporation in the leaves is greater than the water uptake by the roots.
- Evaporation is more rapid in hot, dry or windy conditions.
- The guard cells can close to prevent excessive water loss. **Wilting** of the whole plant can also reduce water loss. The leaves collapse and hang down, which reduces the surface area.

> 1 *By what process does water vapour move out of the leaves?*

Key points

- The loss of water vapour from the surface of plant leaves is known as transpiration.
- Water is lost through the stomata, which open to let in carbon dioxide for photosynthesis.
- Transpiration is more rapid in hot, dry, windy or bright conditions.

Study tip

Remember that the transpiration stream is driven by the loss of water by evaporation out of the stomata.

Practical

Evidence for transpiration

A potometer can be used to show how the uptake of water by a plant changes with different conditions. This gives you a good idea of the amount of water carried through the transpiration stream and lost by evaporation.

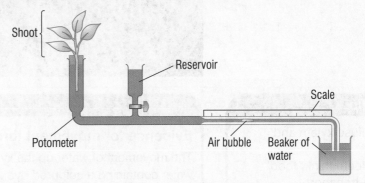

Figure 1 A potometer is used to show the water uptake of a plant under different conditions

> 2 *What conditions could increase the rate of transpiration?*

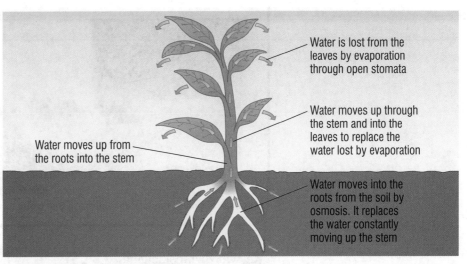

Water is lost from the leaves by evaporation through open stomata

Water moves up through the stem and into the leaves to replace the water lost by evaporation

Water moves up from the roots into the stem

Water moves into the roots from the soil by osmosis. It replaces the water constantly moving up the stem

Key words: transpiration, transpiration stream, wilting

Figure 2 The transpiration stream

Student Book
pages 122–123 **B9.6**

Transport systems in plants

Key points

- Flowering plants have separate transport systems.
- Xylem tissue transports water and mineral ions from the roots to the stems and leaves.
- Phloem tissue transports dissolved sugars from the leaves to the rest of the plant, including the growing regions and storage organs.

⚭ **links**

Revise more on phloem and xylem in 2.5 'Tissues and organs'.

Flowering plants have separate transport systems.

- **Xylem** tissue transports water and mineral ions from the roots to the stem, leaves and flowers.
- The movement of water from the roots through the xylem and out of the leaves is called the transpiration stream.
- **Phloem** tissue carries dissolved sugars from the leaves to the rest of the plant, including the growing regions and the storage organs. This process is called **translocation**.

▐▐▐➤ **1** *What are the names of the two transport tissues in flowering plants?*

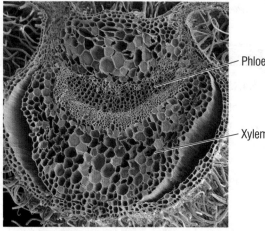

Phloem

Xylem

Figure 1 The phloem and xylem are arranged in vascular bundles in the stem

Study tip

Don't confuse xylem and phloem.
- For **ph**loem think '**f**ood' (sugar) transport.
- For xylem think 'transports water'.

Practical

Evidence for movement through xylem

The movement of water up the xylem can be demonstrated by celery stalks in water containing a coloured dye. After a few hours, slice the stem in several places – coloured circles can be seen where the water and dye have moved through the xylem.

▐▐▐➤ **2** *Suggest how you could use this method to investigate how external conditions affect the rate of transpiration?*

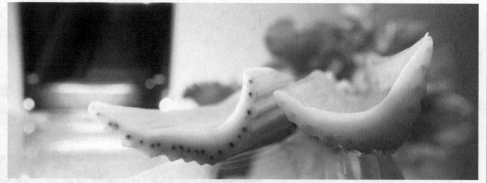

Figure 2 A simple way of demonstrating that water moves up the xylem in celery

Key word: translocation

B9.7 Plant responses

- Plant responses to light, gravity and moisture are known as **tropisms**.
- Plant shoots grow towards light so they can **photosynthesise**. This response is **phototropism**.
- Roots grow down towards gravity. This response is **gravitropism** (geotropism).
- Roots also grow towards water. This response is **hydrotropism**.
- **Auxin** is the hormone that controls phototropism and gravitropism.
- Unequal distribution of auxin causes unequal growth. This results in bending of the shoot or root.

▶ **1** *Why do shoots bend towards light?*

Practical

The effect of light on the growth of seedlings

The effect of one-sided light on the growth of seedlings can be investigated using a simple box with a hole cut in it and cress seedlings growing in a Petri dish.

▶ **2** *Will the shoots grow straight up, away from the hole, or towards the hole?*

1 A normal young bean plant is laid on its side in the dark. Auxin is equally spread through the tissues.

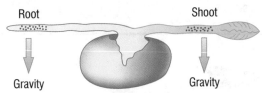

2 In the root, more auxin gathers on the lower side.

In the shoot, more auxin gathers on the lower side.

3 The root grows *more* on the side with *least* auxin, making it bend and grow down towards the force of gravity. When it has grown down, the auxin becomes evenly spread again.

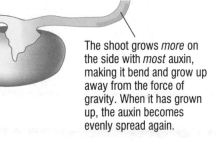

The shoot grows *more* on the side with *most* auxin, making it bend and grow up away from the force of gravity. When it has grown up, the auxin becomes evenly spread again.

Figure 1 Gravitropism (or geotropism) in shoots and roots. The uneven distribution of the hormone auxin causes unequal growth rates, so the roots grow down and the shoots grow up.

Study tip

The action of auxin in gravitropism in shoots and roots is tricky! Unless you are sure about the difference, just say it causes unequal growth of cells on one side which causes the root or shoot to bend.

Key words: tropism, photosynthesise, phototropism, gravitropism, hydrotropism, auxin

Student Book
pages 126–127

B9.8 Making use of plant hormones

- Plant growth hormones are widely used in horticulture as rooting hormones to increase the success of cuttings.
- Plant growth hormones are widely used in agriculture as weed killers, selectively killing broad-leaved weed plants.

⚭ links

Revise more on plant growth hormones in 9.7 'Plant responses'.

- Plant hormones can be used by farmers (**agriculture**) and by gardeners (**horticulture**).
- Plant growth hormones can be used both as weed killers and to stimulate root growth.
- Weed killers (**herbicides**) are used to kill unwanted plants on lawns.
- When cuttings are taken from plants, hormones are used to encourage roots to grow before the cutting is planted.
- Some hormones are used to encourage fruit to ripen.
- If plant hormones are used incorrectly, they can cause damage to the environment, e.g. weed killers may harm other more useful plants.

▶ **1** *Why is it important to use plant hormones correctly in agriculture?*

Practical

The effect of rooting compounds and weed killers on the growth of plants

The effect of rooting hormone can be investigated by taking some cuttings and growing half of them with rooting powder and half without.

The effects of hormone weed killers can be investigated by applying the correct dose to some grass plants and some broad-leaved plants and observing the results.

▶ **2** *Why are broad-leaved plants more likely to be affected by weed killers than narrow-leaved plants?*

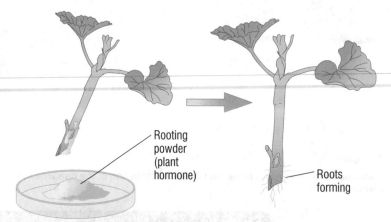

Rooting powder (plant hormone)

Roots forming

Figure 1 Plant growth hormones are used as rooting powder to stimulate growth

Key words: agriculture, horticulture, herbicide

Sexual reproduction in plants

Sexual reproduction in flowering plants involves:

- the flowers which are the plant's sex organs
- the production of male and female gametes
- the transfer of the male gametes (pollen) to the female gametes (**ovules**) in a process called pollination.

Pollination

- The **anther** produces the male gametes in pollen grains. The anther is attached to a **filament** to form a **stamen**.
- The pollen grains are carried by an insect or the wind to the **carpel**, the female part of the flower.
- The carpel is made of the stigma, style and ovary.
- The pollen grains attach to the **stigma** – on top of the **style**.
- The ovules are found in the **ovary** of the flower.
- Pollination occurs once the pollen is attached to the stigma.

> **1** *Where is the male gamete of a flowering plant produced?*

The structure of a flower

Flowers are adapted for either wind or insect pollination. The pollen must be blown or carried efficiently to the stigma.

Wind pollinated flowers have:

- large numbers of small, light pollen grains
- anthers which hang outside the flower
- small **petals**
- large feathery stigmas which hang outside the petals.

Insect pollinated flowers have:

- large, brightly-coloured petals, scent and nectar to attract insects
- anthers and stigmas inside the flower so that insects brush against them when collecting nectar
- relatively few large and sticky pollen grains to attach to insects.

> **2** *Why do some flowers produce nectar?*

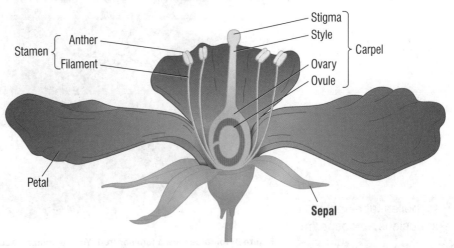

Key words: ovule, anther, filament, stamen, carpel, stigma, style, ovary, petal, sepal

Figure 1 Structure of a typical insect pollinated flower

Student Book
pages 130–131

B9.10

Fertilisation and fruit formation

Key points

- During fertilisation:
  - a pollen tube grows down the style to the ovary
  - nuclei pass from the pollen grain along the pollen tube and fuse with the nuclei in the ovule to fertilise it
  - the resulting zygote develops into an embryo, which forms into a seed with a food store and a tough outer coat
  - the ovary grows into a fruit, which surrounds the seed.

Fertilisation follows the process of pollination.

- During pollination, the pollen grains attach to the stigma on top of a carpel, in which the female gametes (ovules) are located.
- Then a **pollen tube** grows through the carpel's style into the ovule.
- The two **male nuclei** from the pollen grain migrate into the ovule to fertilise the **egg nucleus** and **endosperm nuclei**.

> **1** *How many male nuclei are present in the pollen tube?*

- The resulting zygote develops into an embryo and the endosperm forms a food store.
- The endosperm and the female tissues of the ovule give rise to a seed.
- The ovary then grows into a fruit, which surrounds the seed(s).

> **2** *Which part of the flower grows into the fruit?*

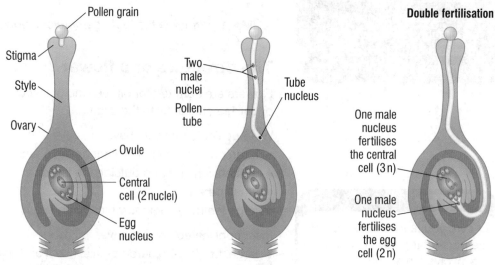

Double fertilisation

Labels: Pollen grain, Stigma, Style, Ovary, Ovule, Central cell (2 nuclei), Egg nucleus, Two male nuclei, Pollen tube, Tube nucleus, One male nucleus fertilises the central cell (3 n), One male nucleus fertilises the egg cell (2 n)

Figure 1 The fertilisation of the nuclei in the ovule by the pollen nuclei

Key words: pollen tube, male nuclei, egg nucleus, endosperm nucleus

Figure 2 Tomatoes are a familiar fruit. You can clearly see the seeds inside the fleshy tissue of the ovary wall.

1. What factors must be controlled in a greenhouse to improve plant growth?

2. Describe the test for starch.

3. What is transported by:
   a xylem?
   b phloem?

4. What is the chemical equation for photosynthesis?

5. Why would there be little point in heating a greenhouse on a summer's day?

6. What is meant by the term 'limiting factor' in photosynthesis?

7. How is the Venus flytrap adapted to live in soil without mineral ions?

8. Explain why plants wilt.

9. Give a use of plant hormones in agriculture.

10. Describe what happens in a root to make it bend down towards the force of gravity.

11. List the stages following pollination up to the development of the fruit.

12. Explain the difference between pollination and fertilisation in a flowering plant.

Study tip

Remember that fertilisation in plants involves two male nuclei.

Chapter checklist	✔	✔	✔
Tick when you have:			
reviewed it after your lesson	✔	☐	☐
revised once – some questions right	✔	✔	☐
revised twice – all questions right	✔	✔	✔
Move on to another topic when you have all three ticks			

Photosynthesis	☐	☐	☐
Limiting factors	☐	☐	☐
How plants use glucose	☐	☐	☐
Exchange in plants	☐	☐	☐
Evaporation and transpiration	☐	☐	☐
Transport systems in plants	☐	☐	☐
Plant responses	☐	☐	☐
Making use of plant hormones	☐	☐	☐
Sexual reproduction in plants	☐	☐	☐
Fertilisation and fruit formation	☐	☐	☐

1 Penicillin is an antibiotic.
  a Explain why doctors prescribe antibiotics? *(2 marks)*
  b Influenza (flu) is caused by a virus. It is difficult to treat diseases caused by a virus. Explain why. *(2 marks)*

In the following question you will be assessed on using good English, organising information clearly and using scientific terms where appropriate.

Penicillin is produced by a fungus. The fungus is grown in fermenters containing nutrients. The graph shows the relationship between the growth of the fungus and the production of penicillin.

  c Discuss the shape of the curves for the growth of fungus and the production of penicillin. Suggest why the production of penicillin does not start immediately. *(6 marks)*

2 Flowering plants reproduce sexually.
  a Look at the photo of a flower. Draw a label to the part of the flower where the male gametes are produced. *(1 mark)*
  b What is the name of the female gamete? *(1 mark)*
  c Where are the female gametes located inside the flower? *(1 mark)*
  d i How is the male gamete transferred from one flower to another flower of this species? *(1 mark)*
    ii Give a reason for your answer to (d) (i) that is visible in the photograph. *(1 mark)*
    iii Give **one** other adaptation the flower may have, which is not visible in the diagram, to ensure the transfer of the male gamete. *(1 mark)*
  e Complete the following sentences:
    There are two male nuclei which travel down a tube to reach the female nuclei. One male nucleus fuses with two female nuclei to form a food store called the _____ . The other male nucleus fuses with the egg cell nucleus in the process of _____ to form the _____ which develops into the _____ . The seeds which then develop are usually found inside a _____ . *(5 marks)*

3 Following a meal your blood sugar rises. During the next few hours the blood sugar returns to normal levels.
  Tick **one** box to answer *each* question.
  a The blood sugar rises because:
    glucose leaves the liver ☐   glucose enters the muscles ☐
    glucose passes into the villi ☐   the muscles are exercising ☐ *(1 mark)*
  b The rise in blood sugar is detected by receptors in the:
    brain ☐   liver ☐
    pancreas ☐   intestine ☐ *(1 mark)*
  c The response to the rise in blood sugar is a **reduction** in the production of:
    ADH ☐   glucagon ☐
    insulin ☐ *(1 mark)*

B10.1

Inheritance

- The nucleus of a cell contains thread-like structures called chromosomes.
- The chromosome threads carry the genes.
- In the nuclei of sex cells (gametes) there is only a single set of chromosomes.
- Therefore, nuclei of male and female sex cells contain one set of genes.

> **1** *Where are genes found?*

- The genetic information from the parents is passed on to the offspring during reproduction. So the offspring cells contain two sets of genes, one set inherited from each parent.
- Different genes control the development of different characteristics of the offspring.
- In most body cells the chromosomes are in pairs. One set came from the female gamete (from the mother) and one set from the male gamete (from the father).

> **2** *What do genes control?*

There are two main causes of variation between individuals of the same kind of organism. **Genetic causes** and **environmental causes** combine to make each individual organism look different.

Key points

- Parents pass on genetic information to their offspring in the sex cells (gametes).
- The genetic information is found in the nucleus of your cells. The nucleus contains chromosomes, and chromosomes carry the genes that control the characteristics of your body.
- Different genes control the development of different characteristics.
- Differences in the characteristics of individuals may be due to genetic causes, environmental causes or both.

Key words: genetic cause, environmental cause

Study tip

One chromosome → many genes → lots of DNA.

B10.2

Types of reproduction

- **Asexual reproduction** does not involve the fusion of gametes (sex cells). All the genetic information comes from one parent. All the offspring are genetically identical to the parent, so there is little variety.
- Identical copies produced by asexual reproduction are called **clones**.
- **Sexual reproduction** involves the fusion of sex cells (gametes). There is a mixing of genetic information, so the offspring show variation.
- In animals, the sex cells are eggs and sperm.
- Offspring produced by sexual reproduction are similar to both parents, but cannot be identical. That is because they have a combination of two sets of genes.

> **1** *Explain which type of reproduction produces genetically identical offspring.*

- Random mixing of genes leads to variation in the offspring. This is important in survival. Some characteristics may give offspring a better chance of surviving difficult conditions.

> **2** *Explain which type of reproduction leads to variation in the offspring.*

Key points

- In asexual reproduction, there is no joining of gametes and only one parent. There is no genetic variety in the offspring.
- The genetically identical offspring of asexual reproduction are known as clones.
- In sexual reproduction, male and female gametes join. The mixture of genetic information from two parents leads to genetic variety in the offspring.
- The different forms of a gene are known as alleles.

∞ links

Revise more on sexual reproduction in plants in 9.9 'Sexual reproduction in plants' and 9.10 'Fertilisation and fruit formation'.

Key words: asexual reproduction, clone, sexual reproduction

B10.3

Genetic and environmental differences

Key points

- The different characteristics between individuals of a family or species may be due to genetic causes, environmental causes or a combination of both.
- Identical twins are clones who share the same genetic material, but even they will never be exactly identical due to differences in their environmental influences.

∞ links

Revise more on producing genetically identical plants in 11.1 'Cloning'.

Revise more on DNA in 10.4 'From Mendel to modern genetics'.

Revise more on how sexual reproduction gives rise to genetic variety in 2.2 'Cell division in sexual reproduction' and 10.2 'Types of reproduction'.

Revise more on the effect of genetic and environmental factors on characteristics in 10.3 'Genetic and environmental differences'.

- Differences in the characteristics of individuals of the same kind (same species) may be due to:
  - differences in the genes they have inherited
  - the conditions in which they have developed
  - a combination of both genetic and environmental causes.

1 *What are the two factors that control some of our characteristics?*

Figure 1 The puppies in this litter have the same parents. The puppies have many similarities but mixing of their parents' genes has led to variations in their appearance. Can you guess what the parents may have looked like?

- Genes are the most important factor in controlling the appearance of an individual.
- Plants may be affected by lack of light, nutrients or space to grow. The weaker plants may have the same genes as the healthier plants but cannot grow well if deprived of nutrients.
- Human development may be affected during pregnancy. If the mother smokes or drinks a lot of alcohol, the baby may have a low birth weight.
- Once animals are born, too much or too little food can alter their characteristics. For example, genes may determine if someone has the potential to be a good athlete. However, training to develop muscles and eating the correct diet will also alter the athlete's body.

2 *Which environmental factors can change a plant's appearance?*

Study tip

Genes control the development of characteristics.
Characteristics may be changed by the environment.

B10.4 # From Mendel to modern genetics

Key points

- In human body cells, the sex chromosomes determine whether you are female (XX) or male (XY).
- Some features are controlled by a single gene.
- Genes can have different forms called alleles.
- Some genes are dominant and some recessive.
- We can construct genetic diagrams to predict characteristics.
- Gregor Mendel was the first person to suggest separately inherited factors, which we now call genes.

- Human beings have 23 pairs of chromosomes. One pair are the **sex chromosomes** – human females have two X chromosomes (XX) and males have an X and a Y chromosome (XY).
- Genes controlling the same characteristic are called alleles.
- If an allele 'masks' the effect of another it is said to be '**dominant**'. The allele where the effect is 'masked' is said to be '**recessive**'.
- Genetic diagrams, including family trees, illustrate how alleles and characteristics are inherited.

▶ **1 Which sex chromosomes are found in human males?**

Genetic terms

Genetic diagrams are biological models which can be constructed to predict and explain the inheritance of particular characteristics. Punnett squares are grids used to insert the alleles' symbols.

It is important to use the correct terminology.

- **Phenotype** – physical appearance of the characteristic, e.g. dimples or no dimples.
- **Genotype** – the genetic make up – which alleles does the individual inherit? **DD**, **Dd** or **dd**.
- **Homozygous** – both alleles are the same **DD** (homozygous dominant) or **dd** (homozygous recessive).
- **Heterozygous** – the two alleles are different **Dd**.
- **Monohybrid inheritance** – the inheritance of a single characteristic controlled by a pair of alleles.

Gregor Mendel observed clear patterns of inheritance in pea plants before anyone had discovered chromosomes. He counted the number of plants with a particular characteristic and recorded his findings carefully. Mendel realised that there are separate units of inheritance.

▶ **2 What do we now call Mendel's units of inheritance?**

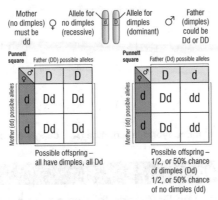

Figure 1 The different forms of genes, known as alleles, can result in the development of quite different characteristics. Genetic diagrams such as these Punnett squares help you explain what is happening and predict what the possible offspring might be like.

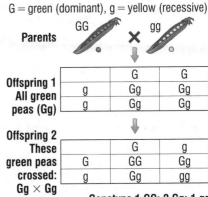

Genotype 1 GG: 2 Gg: 1 gg
Phenotype 3 green peas: 1 yellow pea

Figure 2 Gregor Mendel was the father of modern genetics. His work with peas was not recognised in his lifetime, but now we know just how right he was!

Key words: sex chromosome, dominant, recessive, phenotype, genotype, homozygous, heterozygous, monohybrid inheritance

B10.5 Inheritance in action

Key points

- Chromosomes are made up of large molecules of DNA.
- A gene is a small section of DNA that codes for a particular combination of amino acids which makes a specific protein.
- We can construct genetic diagrams including Punnett squares and family trees to predict inherited characteristics.

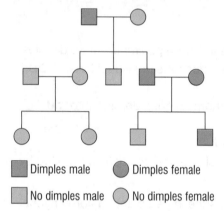

Dimples male
Dimples female
No dimples male
No dimples female

Figure 1 A family tree to show the inheritance of dimples

- **Chromosomes** are made of **DNA** (deoxyribonucleic acid).
- DNA is a very long molecule with strands which are twisted into a double helix structure.
- DNA contains four compounds called bases.
- **Genes** are short sections of DNA with a large number of **bases**, grouped into threes.
- Each gene has the code to make a specific protein.
- A sequence of three bases is the code for a particular amino acid.
- The order of the bases controls the order of the amino acids in the protein.

▶ **1** *How many bases form the code for one amino acid?*

- Family trees and Punnett squares are clear ways to illustrate inheritance. When you trace a family tree, look for evidence of which allele (form of a gene) is dominant and which recessive. If a characteristic is 'hidden' in a generation and appears later, it is controlled by a recessive allele.

▶ **2** *Name a type of genetic diagram.*

Study tip

To improve your grade, make sure you understand how a family tree works. Read the information carefully before answering family tree questions.

To write the best answer in a genetics question you should be able to construct a Punnett square, correctly write in the symbols and use the correct terminology. There are many Punnett square examples on the internet for practice.

Remember, there are only a few possible crosses:

AA × AA, aa × aa, AA × aa, Aa × Aa, Aa × aa, Aa × AA

Try them all out on Punnet squares and write down the ratios of each genotype.

Punnett square 1: two heterozygous organisms (Aa) × (Aa)

	A	a
A	AA	Aa
a	Aa	aa

Genotype: 1 homozygous dominant: 2 heterozygous: 1 homozygous recessive

Ratio: 1 AA : 2 Aa : 1 aa

Phenotype: 3 dangly : 1 attached earlobes

Punnett square 2: heterozygous (Aa) × homozygous recessive (aa)

	A	a
a	Aa	aa
a	Aa	aa

Genotype: 2 heterozygous: 2 homozygous recessive

Ratio: Aa : aa

Phenotype: 1 dangly : 1 attached earlobes

Figure 2 You can use genetic diagrams to show the patterns of monohybrid inheritance (A = dangly earlobes, a = attached earlobes)

Study tip

Three bases on DNA code for one amino acid. Amino acids are joined together to make a protein. It is the particular sequence of amino acids that gives each protein a specific shape and function.

Key words: DNA, bases

B10.6 # Inherited conditions in humans

Key points

- Some disorders are inherited.
- Polydactyly is caused by a dominant allele of a gene and can be inherited from either parent.
- Cystic fibrosis is caused by a recessive allele of a gene and so must be inherited from both parents.
- You can use genetic diagrams to predict how genetic disorders might be inherited and predict the inheritance of genetic disease.

⬤⬤ links

Revise more on how scientists can change the genes in the cells of an organism in 11.3 'Genetic engineering'.
Revise more on how to construct and use genetic diagrams and the patterns of Mendelian inheritance in 10.4 'From Mendel to modern genetics' and 10.5 'Inheritance in action'.

- **Polydactyly** can be passed on by one parent who has the allele.
- If an allele is recessive, the person must inherit two recessive alleles to have the disorder.
- **Cystic fibrosis** is an **inherited disorder** caused by a recessive allele. The allele affects cell membranes and causes the production of thick sticky mucus. The mucus can affect several organs, including the lungs and pancreas.
- A child must inherit a recessive allele from both parents to develop cystic fibrosis. The disorder can be passed on from two parents who don't have cystic fibrosis themselves. The parents are described as **carriers** of the allele.
- By using genetic diagrams, it is possible to see how a **genetic disorder** (or allele) has been inherited and to predict whether future offspring will inherit it.

▶ **1** *Name a genetic disorder which is controlled by a dominant allele.*

- If one parent is heterozygous for polydactyly, each child has a 50% chance of inheriting the disorder.
- If both parents are heterozygous for cystic fibrosis, each child has a 25% chance of inheriting the disorder.
- The outcomes of genetic crosses can be shown on a Punnett square.

▶ **2** *What are the chances of a child having cystic fibrosis if one parent has the disorder and the other parent is heterozygous?*

- It is hoped that in the future some genetic disorders can be cured by **genetic engineering** techniques.

	P	p
p	Pp	pp
p	Pp	pp

50% chance polydactyly, PP or Pp, 50% chance normal pp

Pp = Parent with polydactyly
pp = Normal parent

Figure 1 A genetic diagram (Punnett square) for polydactyly

Both parents are carriers, so Cc

	C	c
C	CC	Cc
c	Cc	cc

Genotype:
25% normal (CC)
50% carriers (Cc)
25% affected by cystic fibrosis (cc)

Phenotype:
3/4, or 75% chance normal
1/4, or 25% chance cystic fibrosis

Figure 2 A genetic diagram (Punnett square) for cystic fibrosis

Key words: polydactyly, cystic fibrosis, inherited disorder, carrier, genetic disorder, genetic engineering

B10.7

More inherited conditions in humans

Key points

- Sickle-cell anaemia is an inherited condition that affects the red blood cells and is caused by a recessive allele.
- Being heterozygous for the sickle-cell allele gives people some protection against malaria compared with people who are homozygous for the dominant normal allele.
- Some inherited conditions are caused by the inheritance of abnormal numbers of chromosomes. For example, Down's syndrome is caused by the presence of an extra chromosome.

Study tip

Learn which type of genes cause genetic disorders.
Dominant: Polydactyly and Huntington's disease
Recessive: Cystic fibrosis and sickle-cell anaemia

Sickle-cell anaemia

- This is a genetic disorder caused by a recessive allele.
- The disorder affects the shape of the red blood cells which cannot carry oxygen efficiently and may block the small blood vessels, causing pain.
- People who are homozygous usually do not survive.
- People who are heterozygous for the **sickle-cell anaemia** gene, have some sickle blood cells. This gives them protection from the malaria **parasite**.
- The majority of the population are homozygous for the dominant gene so their red blood cells have the normal shape. Homozygous dominant people are more likely to catch malaria, which kills many people.

1 *Which cells are affected by sickle-cell anaemia?*

Whole chromosome disorders

- Some inherited conditions are caused by inheritance of abnormal numbers of chromosomes.
- A mistake during meiosis could lead to a cell with too many or too few chromosomes.
- Down's syndrome is caused by the presence of an extra chromosome, 47 instead of 46.
- A child with Down's syndrome could have a range of developmental problems due to the extra chromosome 21.

links
Revise more on meiosis in 2.2 'Cell division in sexual reproduction'.

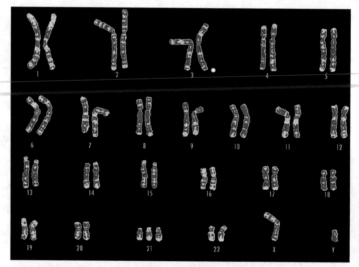

Figure 1 Inheriting an extra chromosome can affect many systems in the body, which is seen clearly when someone is affected by Down's syndrome

Key words: sickle-cell anaemia, parasite

B10.8 Screening for genetic disease

Screening embryos

- Embryo screening involves tests to diagnose genetic disorders before the baby is born.
- The results of the test may give the parents choices. Sometimes the parents decide to terminate the pregnancy. Other parents decide this is not ethical but can prepare for the delivery of an affected baby.
- In IVF the embryos are screened and only healthy embryos are implanted into the mother. Embryos carrying faulty genes are destroyed and some people think this is unethical.

Gene probes

- DNA is isolated from the embryo cells.
- A **gene probe** that will bind on to the gene for a specific disorder is produced.
- The gene probe has a fluorescent chemical attached to it.
- The probe is added to a mixture containing the DNA sample from the embryo.
- UV light is used to detect the probe.
- If the probes have attached to the faulty allele and fluoresce, the embryo or fetus is affected by the condition.

> 1 What is a gene probe?

Concerns about embryo screening include:
- the risk of miscarriage
- the reliability of the information of the screening process as sometimes there can be **false positive** or **false negative** results
- decisions about terminating pregnancy.

> 2 What is embryo screening?

Key points

- Cells from embryos and fetuses can be screened for the alleles that cause many genetic disorders using gene probes.
- Concerns about embryo and fetal screening include the risk of miscarriage, the reliability of the screening procedure, and the decisions that have to be made about whether or not to terminate a pregnancy.

Study tip

To improve your grade, always look at both sides of an argument about the use of embryos and try to write a balanced account. Your conclusion should be based on the argument you have given.

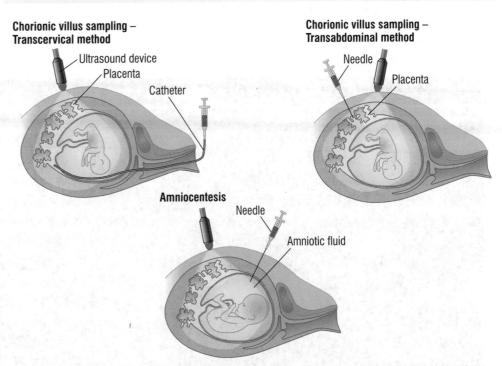

Figure 1 Amniocentesis and chorionic villus sampling enable us to take cells from a developing fetus. The cells can then be screened for genetic diseases.

Key words: gene probe, false positive, false negative

1 What is meant by the term 'phenotype'?

2 What causes Down's syndrome?

3 Name the cell which results from the fusion of the male and female gamete.

4 What molecule are genes made of?

5 What are 'alleles'?

6 Why does sexual reproduction result in variation?

7 Explain why offspring produced by asexual reproduction are genetically identical.

8 What is meant by a 'heterozygous' individual?

9 What are the chances of a child having polydactyly if one parent is heterozygous and the other parent is homozygous recessive?

10 Explain why two parents without sickle-cell anaemia can have a child with the condition.

11 How does a gene control the production of a protein?

> **Study tip**
>
> Ensure that you understand why one type of reproduction results in variation and the other doesn't. It is simply that in sexual reproduction genes are inherited from two parents. However, in asexual (no sex) reproduction there is only one parent, so variation is impossible!

Chapter checklist

Tick when you have:

reviewed it after your lesson	✔	☐	☐
revised once – some questions right	✔	✔	☐
revised twice – all questions right	✔	✔	✔

Move on to another topic when you have all three ticks

	✔	✔	✔
Inheritance	☐	☐	☐
Types of reproduction	☐	☐	☐
Genetic and environmental differences	☐	☐	☐
From Mendel to modern genetics	☐	☐	☐
Inheritance in action	☐	☐	☐
Inherited conditions in humans	☐	☐	☐
More inherited conditions in humans	☐	☐	☐
Screening for genetic disease	☐	☐	☐

B11.1

Cloning 🔵

- Individuals that are genetically identical to their parents are known as '**clones**'.
- It is much more difficult to clone animals than it is to clone plants.
- Cloning is used to produce new individuals that are useful in farming and agriculture.
- In plants, the process of cloning can be cheap and effective. Plants can be cloned by taking cuttings and growing them.
- Taking small groups of cells from part of a plant and growing them under special conditions (**tissue culture**) is more expensive. A mass of identical plant cells is a **callus**. Tissue culture can be used to reproduce large numbers of a rare or top-quality plant.

⏩ **1** *Name a quick, cheap way of cloning plants.*

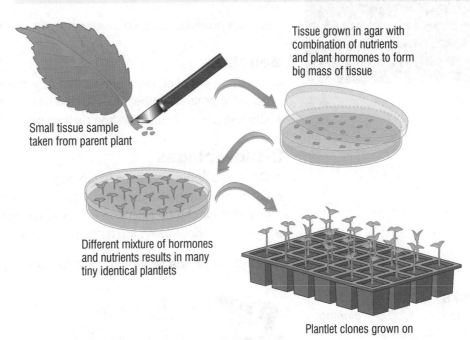

Tissue grown in agar with combination of nutrients and plant hormones to form big mass of tissue

Small tissue sample taken from parent plant

Different mixture of hormones and nutrients results in many tiny identical plantlets

Plantlet clones grown on

Figure 1 Tissue culture makes it possible to produce thousands of identical plants quickly and easily from one small tissue sample

- Embryo transplants are used to clone animals. In this process an embryo with unspecialised cells is split into smaller groups of cells. Each group of genetically identical cells is transplanted and allowed to develop in a host animal.
- Sometimes animals or plants are **genetically modified** to produce useful substances before they are cloned.

⏩ **2** *Suggest why is it more difficult to successfully clone animals than plants.*

Key points

- A modern technique for cloning plants is tissue culture using small groups of cells taken from part of the original plant.
- Transplanting cloned embryos involves splitting apart cells from a developing animal embryo before they become specialised and then transplanting the identical embryos into host mothers.
- Animals and plants that are cloned are chosen because of their high quality, for example in terms of their resistance to disease or high milk yield.

🔗 links

Revise more on cloning embryos in 11.2 'Adult cell cloning'.

Study tip

Make sure you know why clones are identical to their parents.
Remember that clones have identical genetic information to each other and to the nucleus of the single parent.
Learn **how** the different types of cloning work.
If you only know the names of the types of cloning you could lose marks.

Key words: clone, tissue culture, callus, genetically modified

B11.2 Adult cell cloning

Key points

Key points

- In adult cell cloning, the nucleus of a cell from an adult animal is transferred to an empty egg cell from another animal. A small electric shock causes the egg cell to begin to divide and starts embryo development. The embryo is then placed in the womb of a third animal to develop.

- The animal that is born is genetically identical to the animal that donated the original cell.

- In **adult cell cloning** the nucleus of an adult cell, e.g. a skin cell, replaces the nucleus of an egg cell.
- First the nucleus is removed from an unfertilised egg cell. The nucleus is removed from the skin cell and placed inside the 'empty' egg cell.
- The new cell is given an electric shock which causes it to start to divide. The ball of cells is called an embryo.
- The embryo is genetically identical to the adult skin cell.
- Once the embryo has developed into a ball of cells it is inserted into the womb of a host mother.
- Dolly the sheep was produced by adult cell cloning in 1997.

⫸ **1** *Name the two cells needed in adult cell cloning.*

There are benefits, but also disadvantages, of adult cell cloning:

Benefits

- Development of cloned animals that have been genetically engineered to produce valuable proteins in their milk. These have uses in medicine.
- Cloning can save animals from extinction.

Disadvantages

- Concerns about the ethics of cloning.
- Cloning limits the variation in a population (limits the gene pool). This can be a problem for natural selection if the environment changes.
- Concerns about using the technique to clone humans in the future.

⫸ **2** *Give one benefit of adult cell cloning.*

⬯ links

Revise more on adult cell cloning in 11.4 'Making choices about genetic technology'.

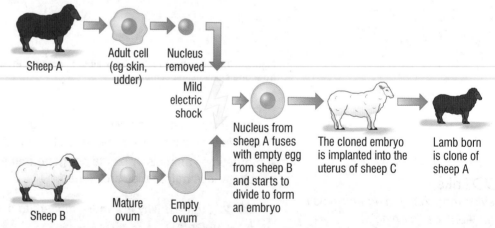

Sheep A → Adult cell (eg skin, udder) → Nucleus removed

Mild electric shock

Sheep B → Mature ovum → Empty ovum → Nucleus from sheep A fuses with empty egg from sheep B and starts to divide to form an embryo → The cloned embryo is implanted into the uterus of sheep C → Lamb born is clone of sheep A

Figure 1 Adult cell cloning is still a very difficult technique – but scientists hope it may bring benefits in the future

Study tip

Plants can be cloned by tissue culture. Animals can be cloned by dividing embryos or by adult cell cloning.

Key word: adult cell cloning

B11.3

Genetic engineering

Key points

- Genes can be transferred to the cells of animals and plants at an early stage of their development so they develop desired characteristics. This is genetic engineering.

- In genetic engineering, genes from the chromosomes of humans and other organisms can be 'cut out' using enzymes and transferred to the cells of bacteria and other organisms using a vector, which is usually a bacterial plasmid or a virus.

- Crops that have had their genes modified are known as genetically modified (GM) crops. GM crops often have improved resistance to insect attack or herbicides and generally produce a higher yield.

links

Revise more on insulin to treat diabetes in 7.8 'Treating diabetes'.

- Genetic engineering involves changing the genetic make-up of an organism.

- Genes can be transferred to the cells of animals, plants or microorganisms at an early stage in their development.

- A gene is 'cut out' of the chromosome of an organism using an enzyme. The gene is then placed in the chromosome of another organism. A vector (carrier) such as a plasmid or virus may be used to transfer the gene.

- The genes may be placed in an organism of the same species to give it a 'desired' characteristic.

- Sometimes genes are placed in a different species, such as a bacterium. For example, the gene to produce insulin in humans can be placed in bacteria. Then the bacteria can produce large quantities of insulin to treat diabetes.

> **1** *What is used to cut genes out of chromosomes?*

- New genes can be transferred to crop plants.
- Crops with changed genes are called **genetically modified (GM) crop** plants.
- GM crops may make their own **pesticide**, or be herbicide-resistant, and usually have increased yields.

> **2** *Why do GM crops often give higher yields than traditional crops?*

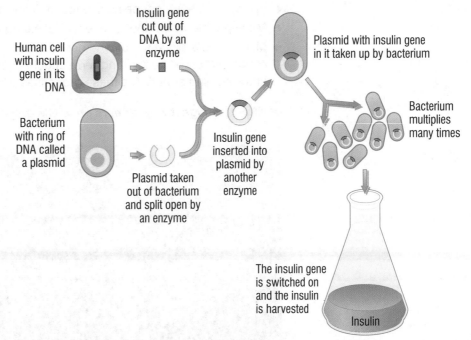

Figure 1 The principles of genetic engineering. A bacterial cell receives a gene from a human being so it makes a human protein – in this case, the human hormone insulin.

Study tip

Cloning and genetic engineering are different! Learn the techniques for both processes.

Key words: genetically modified crop (GM crop), pesticide

Making choices about genetic technology

There are many advantages, but also disadvantages, in using cloning and genetic engineering.

Advantages

● Cloning cattle can produce herds of cattle with useful characteristics.
● Adult cell cloning may be used to make copies of the best animals, e.g. race horses.
● If a person has a faulty gene, they may have a genetic disorder. If the correct gene can be transferred to the person, they could be cured.
● Several medical drugs have been produced by genetic engineering, such as insulin and antibodies.
● GM crops include ones which are resistant to herbicides or to insects.

Disadvantages

● GM crops have a bigger yield, but farmers have to buy new GM seed every year because the crops are infertile.
● Some people are concerned about accidentally introducing genes into wild flower populations.
● Insects which are not pests may be affected by GM crops.
● Many people worry about the effect of eating GM crops on human health.
● Many people argue about whether or not cloning and genetic engineering are ethical. What will be the long-term effects? Will we create new organisms that we know nothing about? Are these processes ethically correct?

1 *Suggest why farmers grow GM crops.*

Figure 1 Varieties of GM rice have been developed to help solve the problem of blindness in children who lack vitamin A in their diet. Yellow beta carotene is needed to make vitamin A in the body. The amount of beta carotene in golden rice and golden rice 2 is reflected in the depth of colour of the rice.

Study tip

If you are hoping to improve your grade, you should always look for the advantages and disadvantages of cloning or genetic engineering and then write a conclusion based on your knowledge and the evidence given in the question.

links
Revise more on GM crops in 11.3 'Genetic engineering'.

1 What is a clone?

2 Some humans are natural clones. Explain who are clones and why.

3 How can plants be cloned quickly?

4 What cloning process is used to produce large numbers of a rare plant?

5 What is meant by 'genetically modified'?

6 What is 'genetic engineering'?

> **Study tip**
>
> Remember that genes are cut out of chromosomes using **enzymes**. This is a chemical process.

7 Give three uses of genetic engineering.

8 Describe how calf embryos could be cloned.

9 Cattle could be left to breed naturally. Why might farmers decide to use embryo cloning?

10 A fish gene is used to produce GM tomatoes. These tomatoes last longer. Describe how the tomato plant is genetically engineered.

Chapter checklist		✓ ✓ ✓
Tick when you have:		
reviewed it after your lesson	✓ ☐ ☐	Cloning ☐ ☐ ☐
revised once – some questions right	✓ ✓ ☐	Adult cell cloning ☐ ☐ ☐
revised twice – all questions right	✓ ✓ ✓	Genetic engineering ☐ ☐ ☐
Move on to another topic when you have all three ticks		Making choices about genetic technology ☐ ☐ ☐

B12.1 Adapt and survive

Key points

- Organisms need a supply of materials from their surroundings and from other living organisms to survive and reproduce.
- Organisms, including microorganisms, have features (adaptations) that enable them to survive in the conditions in which they normally live.
- Extremophiles have adaptations that enable them to live in environments with extreme conditions of salt, temperature or pressure.

Study tip

Practise recognising plant and animal adaptations related to where they live. You may be asked to do this in your examination.

- To survive and reproduce, organisms require materials from their surroundings and from the other organisms living there.
- Plants need light, carbon dioxide, water, oxygen and nutrients, such as mineral ions, from the soil.
- Animals need food from other organisms, water and oxygen.
- Different microorganisms need different materials. Some microorganisms are like plants, others are like animals, and some do not need oxygen or light to survive.
- Special features of organisms are called **adaptations**.
- Adaptations allow organisms to survive in a particular habitat, even when the conditions are extreme, e.g. extremely hot, very salty or at high pressure.

⟫ **1** *What is meant by an 'adaptation'?*

- Plants are adapted to obtain light and other materials efficiently in order to make food by photosynthesis.
- Animals may be plant eating (**herbivores**) or eat other animals (**carnivores**). Their mouthparts are adapted to their diet.
- Most organisms live in temperatures below 40°C so their enzymes can work.
- **Extremophiles** are organisms which are adapted to live in conditions where enzymes won't usually work because they would denature.

⟫ **2** *What are extremophiles?*

⚬⚬ links

Revise more on animal adaptations in 12.2 'Adaptations in animals'.

Key words: adaptation, herbivore, carnivore, extremophile

B12.2 Adaptations in animals

Key points

- All living things have adaptations that help them to survive in the conditions where they live.
- Adaptations include:
  - structural adaptations such as the shape and colour of the organism
  - behavioural adaptations such as migration
  - functional adaptations of processes such as reproduction and metabolism.

⚬⚬ links

You can read more about surface area to volume ratio in 1.7 'Exchanging materials'.

Key word: predator

- If animals were not adapted to survive in the areas they live in, they would die.
- Animals in cold climates (e.g. in the Arctic) have thick fur and fat under the skin (blubber) to keep them warm.
- Some animals in the Arctic (e.g. Arctic fox, Arctic hare) are white in the winter and brown in the summer. This means that they are camouflaged so they are not easily seen. Both **predators** and prey may be camouflaged.
- Bigger animals have smaller surface areas compared to their volume. This means that they can conserve energy more easily but it is also more difficult to cool down.

⟫ **1** *Why do large animals find it difficult to cool down?*

- In hot dry conditions (desert) animals are adapted to conserve water and to stop them getting too hot. Animals in the desert may hunt or feed at night so that they remain cool during the day.

⟫ **2** *Why do some desert animals shelter during the day?*

Study tip

Remember that animals living in very cold conditions often have a low surface area to volume ratio. This means there is less area for heat loss. The opposite can be true in hot climates.

Student Book
pages 166–167

B12.3 Adaptations in plants

Key points

- Plants lose water vapour from the surface of their leaves.
- Plant adaptations for surviving in dry conditions include reducing the surface area of the leaves, having water-storage tissues and growing extensive root systems.

- Plants need light, water, space and nutrients to survive.
- Plants need to collect and conserve water. They can lose water as water vapour through holes in the leaves called stomata.
- Water can be collected if the plant has an extensive root system.
- Water can be conserved if the plant has very small or waxy leaves. A plant might have a swollen stem to store the water.
- In dry conditions, e.g. in deserts, plants (such as cacti) have become very well adapted to conserve water. Others (such as the mesquite tree) have adapted to collect water using extensive root systems.
- Plants are eaten by animals. Some plants have developed thorns, poisonous chemicals and warning colours to put animals off.

> **1** *List the ways a plant can conserve water.*

> **2** *Give one way plants are protected from being eaten by animals.*

Study tip

Remember that plants need their stomata open to exchange gases for photosynthesis and respiration. However, this leads to loss of water by evaporation, so desert plants have adaptations to conserve water.

∞ links
Revise more on transport in plants and transpiration in 9.5 'Evaporation and transpiration' and 9.6 'Transport systems in plants'.

Figure 1 Cacti are well adapted to conserve water and to stop animals eating them

Student Book
pages 168–169

B12.4 Competition in animals

Key points

- Animals compete with each other for food, territories and mates.
- Animals have adaptations that make them successful competitors.

- Animals are in **competition** with each other for water, food, space, mates and breeding sites.
- An animal's **territory** will be large enough to find water, food and have space for breeding.
- Predators compete with their prey, as they want to eat them.
- Predators and prey may be camouflaged, so that they are less easy to see.
- Prey animals compete with each other to escape from the predators and to find food for themselves.
- Some animals, e.g. caterpillars, may be poisonous and have warning colours so that they are not eaten.

> **1** *Why do animals need a territory?*

> **2** *Some caterpillars are not poisonous but predators avoid them. Suggest why.*

Study tip

Make a list of all the possible ways predators and prey might be adapted to compete and survive. Start with warning colours, camouflage, speed and horns. Explain why they are good adaptations.

Learn to look at an animal and spot the adaptations that make it a successful competitor.

Key words: competition, territory

Student Book
pages 170–171 **B12.5**

Competition in plants

Key points

- Plants often compete with each other for light, for space, for water and for nutrients (minerals) from the soil.
- Plants have many adaptations that make them good competitors.

Figure 1 Clover makes its own nitrates. This helps it to outcompete the grass, which has to take its minerals from the soil.

Study tip

Plants compete for space, light, water and mineral ions. Animals compete for food, mates and territory.

- All plants compete for water, nutrients and light. For example, in woodland some smaller plants (e.g. snowdrops) flower before the trees are in leaf. This ensures they get enough light, space, water and nutrients.
- Plants which grow deep roots can reach underground water better than those with shallow roots.
- Some plants spread their seeds over a wide area so that they do not compete with themselves. Some of these plants use:
  - animals to spread their fruits and seeds
  - the wind (e.g. sycamore) or mini-explosions (e.g. broom) to spread their seeds.

Figure 2 The light seeds and fluffy parachutes of dandelion mean they are spread widely and compete very successfully

1 *Why do plants try to spread their seeds as far as possible?*

Practical

Investigating competition in plants

The development in two trays of cress seeds can be compared – one crowded and one spread out. Keep all other conditions identical. After a few days the differences in the growth of the seedlings are recorded.

2 *Suggest the factors the seedlings are competing for.*

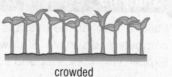

crowded

spread out

B12.6 Adaptations in parasites

Key points

- Parasites are adapted for living on or inside their hosts.
- Fleas are adapted to live among animal hair and take blood meals.
- Tapeworms are adapted for life inside the gut of their hosts.
- The malaria parasite has a number of different forms that are adapted to living in different regions of both mosquitoes and humans.

⟱ **1** *What prevents the tapeworm being expelled from a host's intestine?*

⟱ **2** *What are the four forms of the malaria parasite?*

Parasites are adapted for living on or inside their hosts.

Organism	Adaptation	Purpose of adaptation
Flea – lives amongst hairs of mammals	Sharp, sucking mouthparts	To suck blood from host
	Flattened body	Difficult to dislodge
	Hard body	Not damaged when animal scratches
	Long legs	Can jump from host to host
Tapeworm – lives inside the intestines of mammals and other animals	Hooks and suckers	Holds on to intestine of host
	Long flattened body without a gut	Large surface area for absorbing soluble food from host
	Segments	Produce large numbers of eggs using food absorbed from host
	Thick cuticle	Protects against digestive enzymes of host
Malaria parasite – transferred to humans by mosquito	Several forms in life cycle – gametocytes, sporozoites, merozoites and schizonts	Each form is specialised to live in different parts of the mosquito or human

The malaria parasite (*Plasmodium*) has several stages in its life cycle.

- **Gametocytes** are found in human blood and pass to the salivary glands of the mosquito when it bites the person.
- **Sporozoites** are produced in the salivary glands from gametocytes and are then passed to the blood of humans when they are bitten by the mosquito. The blood carries the sporozoites to the person's liver and they enter the liver cells.
- **Merozoites** are formed when sporozoites divide asexually in the liver. Merozoites leave the liver and enter red blood cells where some turn into schizonts.
- **Schizonts** burst out of red blood cells (causing fever) and releasing more merozoites. Some merozoites reproduce sexually to form gametocytes.

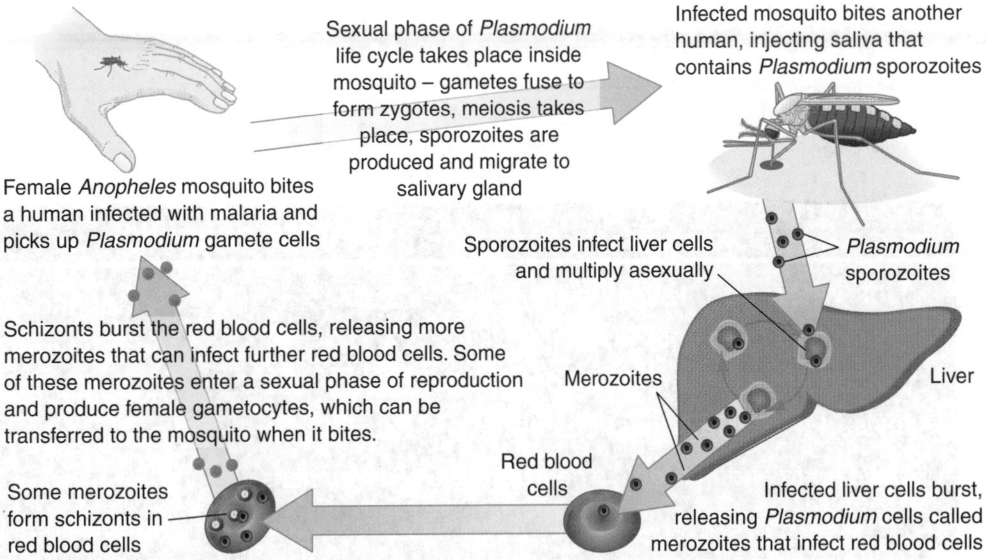

⌾⌾ links

Revise more on the protective effect of sickle-cell anaemia in 10.7 'More inherited conditions in humans'.

Key words: parasite, gametocyte, sporozoite, merozoite, schizont

Figure 1 *Plasmodium* is adapted to live both in mosquito guts and salivary glands and in human liver and blood cells at different times during its complex life cycle

Sexual phase of *Plasmodium* life cycle takes place inside mosquito – gametes fuse to form zygotes, meiosis takes place, sporozoites are produced and migrate to salivary gland

Infected mosquito bites another human, injecting saliva that contains *Plasmodium* sporozoites

Female *Anopheles* mosquito bites a human infected with malaria and picks up *Plasmodium* gamete cells

Sporozoites infect liver cells and multiply asexually

Plasmodium sporozoites

Schizonts burst the red blood cells, releasing more merozoites that can infect further red blood cells. Some of these merozoites enter a sexual phase of reproduction and produce female gametocytes, which can be transferred to the mosquito when it bites.

Merozoites

Liver

Red blood cells

Some merozoites form schizonts in red blood cells

Infected liver cells burst, releasing *Plasmodium* cells called merozoites that infect red blood cells

1. Why are adaptations important?

2. What is meant by 'competition'?

3. What do animals compete for?

4. Suggest why small forest plants produce flowers before the trees produce leaves?

5. What is camouflage and why is it important?

6. List ways in which some plants are adapted to conserve water.

7. Suggest ways a flea is adapted to living in the fur of mammals.

8. A tapeworm does not have a gut. Explain why.

9. Why do tapeworms produce so many eggs in their segments?

10. Where are the four forms of the malaria parasite found?

Study tip

To improve your grade, read all the information given about adaptations and relate these to where the animal or plant lives. Fur colour may aid camouflage, but fur can also prevent energy loss. Make sure your answer is in the correct context.

Chapter checklist

Tick when you have:

reviewed it after your lesson ☑ ☐ ☐

revised once – some questions right ☑ ☑ ☐

revised twice – all questions right ☑ ☑ ☑

Move on to another topic when you have all three ticks

Adapt and survive	☐	☐	☐
Adaptations in animals	☐	☐	☐
Adaptations in plants	☐	☐	☐
Competition in animals	☐	☐	☐
Competition in plants	☐	☐	☐
Adaptations in parasites	☐	☐	☐

1 Glycogen is an important storage compound found in humans.

   a Where is glycogen stored? *(1 mark)*

Glycogen can be converted into glucose.

   b Name the type of chemical that converts glycogen to glucose. *(1 mark)*

   c There are several genetic diseases which cause problems with glycogen storage. These diseases are caused by recessive alleles.

     In one type of glycogen storage disease, glycogen is not converted to glucose.

     The dominant allele (G) allows glycogen to be converted to glucose. The recessive allele (g) does not allow the conversion of glycogen and glucose.

     Construct a genetic diagram to show how two parents without the disease can have a child with glycogen storage disease. *(4 marks)*

   d The gender (sex) of humans is determined by the X and Y chromosomes.

     Give the combinations of these chromosomes for:

     i a male human

     ii a female human. *(2 marks)*

   e In another type of glycogen storage disease the recessive allele is found on the X chromosome. This disease is usually restricted to males and is rarely found in females. Suggest why. *(3 marks)*

2 *In this question you will be assessed on using good English, organising information clearly and using scientific terms where appropriate.*

About 25% of the world's food crops are destroyed every year through insect attack.
The corn borer is an insect that eats corn.

Genetic modification has been used to make a variety of corn that is resistant to the corn borer insect.

The GM corn has a gene from a bacterium which causes it to produce a low level of a bacterial protein. This protein is poisonous to the corn borer. The insect is killed when it eats the maize.

   a Explain how the non-GM corn is modified and how it then produces the bacterial protein. *(6 marks)*

   b Use the information about the GM corn and your own knowledge to evaluate the use of the GM corn compared with non-GM corn. *(4 marks)*

3 Organisms are adapted to live in their environment.

   a **i** Give an example of a structural adaptation in plants. *(1 mark)*

     ii Give an example of a behavioural adaptation in birds. *(1 mark)*

   b Some parasites are adapted to live inside their hosts. Tapeworms can live inside the intestine of mammals. The tapeworm has a flat body, a thick cuticle and a head with hooks and suckers.

     Explain the value of these adaptations to the tapeworm:

     i Flat body. *(2 marks)*

     ii Thick cuticle. *(2 marks)*

     iii Head with hooks and suckers. *(2 marks)*

   c Malaria is caused by a single-celled organism. The malaria parasite is transmitted to humans by mosquitoes.

     When the mosquito bites the human's skin it injects saliva into the blood vessels. The saliva contains sporozoites which are one form of the malaria parasite.

     Using the terms below, describe what happens inside the human following a mosquito bite and what causes the fever associated with malaria. *(6 marks)*

merozoites	sporozoites	schizonts

Study tip

Remember there are only a few combinations of alleles. In this example use the letters given – G and g. If you decide to use your own letters, you must give a key. Do not be put off by part (e). This is an application of knowledge about genetics and sex determination – you need to remember that males only have one X chromosome.

Study tip

For question 2, you need to tell the whole story and use scientific terms which are not in the question. You must explain how the gene is transferred into the corn and then describe how the DNA code in the gene determines the order of amino acids in the protein.

Study tip

When you see the word 'evaluate' you must look for two sides of an argument or the pros and cons of a process. In question 2(b), you should look for the advantages and disadvantages of GM corn versus non-GM corn. Always give a conclusion with a reason for your decision.

Study tip

If you are given terms to use, make sure you include all of them in your answer.

Student Book
pages 176–177

B13.1

Organisms in their environment

Key points

- There are relationships both within and between communities of living organisms.
- Factors that may affect the distribution of living organisms include changes in:
  - the numbers or types of competitor organisms
  - temperature
  - nutrients
  - the amount of light
  - the availability of water
  - the availability of oxygen and carbon dioxide
  - the availability of nest sites, shelter and appropriate habitats.

∞ **links**

Revise more on competition in 12.4 'Competition in animals' and 12.5 'Competition in plants'.

Study tip

If you are given data about the distribution of organisms, look for reasons why plants might not be able to grow there. Plants supply food for animals so fewer plants results in fewer animals.

∞ **links**

Revise more on measuring oxygen levels in aquatic environments in 13.4 'Measuring environmental change'.

Living organisms form communities. It is important to understand the relationships within and between these communities. These relationships can be influenced by external factors. Physical factors that may affect the distribution of organisms are:

- **Temperature** – for example, arctic plants are small which limits the number of plant eaters which can survive in the area.
- **Availability of nutrients** – most plants struggle to grow when mineral ions are in short supply and again few animals will survive in that area.
- **Amount of light** – few plants live on a forest floor because the light is blocked out by the trees. Shaded plants often have broader leaves or more chlorophyll.
- **Availability of water** – water is important for all organisms so few will live in a desert. If it rains in the desert, then plants grow and produce flowers and seeds very quickly. Then there will be food for animals.
- **Availability of oxygen** –animals living in water can be affected by the levels of dissolved oxygen. Some invertebrates can live at very low oxygen levels, but most fish need relatively high levels of oxygen to be dissolved in the water.
- **Availability of carbon dioxide** – lack of carbon dioxide will affect plant growth and consequently the food available for animals.
- **Availability of nesting sites, shelter and appropriate habitats** – to feed and breed successfully organisms need a suitable place to live. Loss of nesting sites causes a decrease in bird populations.

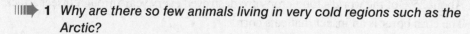

> **1** *Why are there so few animals living in very cold regions such as the Arctic?*

Living factors can change communities

- If a new predator enters a habitat, it will reduce the numbers of prey animals. Then there will be less food for all the carnivores and their numbers may decrease.
- If more herbivores are eaten, this may allow more grass to grow.
- Rabbits are herbivores that breed rapidly. Rabbits caused the extinction of other grass-eating herbivores in Australia when they were introduced.

> **2** *How do new predators change communities?*

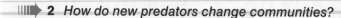

Figure 1 Snow leopards are one of the rarest big cats. They live in cold, high-altitude environments where there are not many plants, and so there are very few herbivores for the snow leopards to hunt.

B13.2 Measuring the distribution of organisms

Key points

- You can get quantitative data on the distribution of organisms in the environment using:
  - random sampling with quadrats
  - sampling along a transect.
- Determining the range, mean, median and mode of your data will help you to understand more about the distribution of living organisms.

Study tip

Remember – you sample with quadrats along a transect to see a change in species distribution in a line from A to B.

You sample with quadrats on coordinates from a random number generator to count the number of a species in an area.

Quantitative data can be used to describe how physical factors might be affecting the distribution of organisms in a particular habitat. Quantitative data can be obtained by:

- random **quantitative sampling** using a quadrat
- sampling along a **transect**.

A **quadrat** is a square frame made of metal or wood which may be subdivided into a grid. If several quadrats are placed randomly in a field, the investigator can count the number of a particular type of plant or animal in each quadrat. This can be used to estimate the number of, for example, daisies in the whole field.

- **Sample size** is important. In a large field enough random quadrats must be placed to be sure the sample is representative of the whole field.
- An estimate of the number of, for example, daisies is usually given as a **mean** (average) per square metre.

A transect is not random. A line is marked between two points, e.g. from the top of a rocky shore down to the sea. A quadrat can be placed every five metres along the line and the organisms counted. Physical factors could also be measured at each quadrat point. This method supplies a lot of information about the habitat and the organisms in it.

⟹ **1** *What is a quadrat?*

⟹ **2** *What is a transect?*

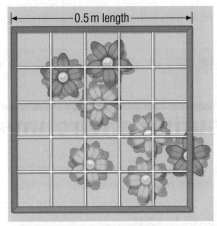

Figure 1 With plants partly covered by the quadrat, decide whether they are in or out and *stick to it*. In this quadrat, you have six or seven plants per 0.25 m² (that's 24 or 28 plants per square metre), depending on the way you count.

Study tip

Make sure you know the difference between:
- mean (the sum of the values divided by the number of values)
- median (the middle value of the range)
- mode (the most frequently occurring value).

Key words: quantitative sampling, transect, quadrat, sample size, mean, range, median, mode

 Maths skills – Finding the range, the mean, the median and the mode

You need to understand the terms **range**, mean, **median** and **mode** when recording quantitative data.

The following readings are the numbers of daisies counted in 11 quadrats of 1 m²:

10 11 20 15 11 10 18 20 10 13 5

The **range** is the difference between the minimum and maximum readings: in this case the range of the daisies is 20 − 5 = 15 per m².

The **mean** is the sum of the readings divided by the number of readings taken: in this case the mean is 143 ÷ 11 = 13 per m².

The **median** is the middle value of the readings when written in order:

5 10 10 10 11 11 13 15 18 20 20

In this case it is the sixth value out of the 11 readings, so the median is 11 per m².

The **mode** is the reading which appears the most frequently: in this case the mode is 10 per m².

B13.3

How valid is the data?

Key points

- Different methods can be used to collect environmental data.
- Repeatability, reproducibility and validity must be considered carefully as it is difficult to control variables in fieldwork.
- Sample size is an important factor in the repeatability, reproducibility and validity of data.

Study tip

You will improve your grade if you can use all the mathematical terms involved in data analysis and make sure you understand the difference between repeatability and reproducibility.

- Investigations about the distribution of organisms in their environment can be very difficult. That is because they are often carried out over a long time and not all variables can be controlled.
- If a transect is made at a beach during the morning, a comparative investigation must be done at the same time of day even if it is two months later. The time of day is a control variable. We can control this variable. In a **valid** investigation all possible **variables** must be controlled.
- A measurement is **repeatable** if the original experimenter repeats the investigation using the same method and equipment and obtains the same results. However, sometimes the experimenter may be making the same mistake every time and get repeatable results! So it may also be necessary to check the results to ensure they are **reproducible**.
- A measurement is reproducible if the investigation is repeated by another person, or by using different equipment or techniques, and the same results are obtained.

> **1** *What is meant by repeatable results?*

- Sample size is an important factor in obtaining valid, repeatable and reproducible results. If the sample is too small, it may not be representative. So the larger the sample size, the more trust we can have in the data generated in an environmental investigation.

> **2** *How can you make sure an investigation is valid?*

Key words: valid, variable, repeatable, reproducible

B13.4

Measuring environmental change

Key points

- The distribution of living things is affected by both living and non-living factors.
- Environmental changes can be measured using non-living indicators such as oxygen levels, temperature and rainfall.
- Living organisms can be used as indicators of environmental change and pollution; for example, lichens for air pollution, invertebrate animals for water pollution and dissolved oxygen levels.

Key words: indicator, biotic index of water cleanliness

- Animals and plants are affected by their environment. If the environment changes, the organisms may not be able to live there any more.
- Non-living factors which might change include: temperature, rainfall, light and oxygen levels in water.
- Living factors which might change include: arrival of a new predator or disease, or the introduction of new plants which might provide new food or habitats.

> **1** *Name three non-living environmental factors.*

Pollution indicators and monitoring

- Lichens indicate the level of air pollution, particularly sulfur dioxide. The more species of lichen growing, the cleaner the air. They are an example of an **indicator** species, which provides us with evidence of changes in environmental pollution levels.
- Freshwater invertebrates indicate the level of water pollution in the same way, in particular the concentration of dissolved oxygen in the water. The wider the range of these invertebrates, the cleaner the water in the stream, river or pond. Some freshwater invertebrates will only live in polluted water.
- Equipment such as rain gauges, thermometers, pH and oxygen sensors and dataloggers can be used to monitor non-living changes in the environment.
- The **biotic index of water cleanliness** is a measure of how clean water is by studying the type and numbers of living organisms found in it.

Figure 1 Lichens grow well where the air is clean. In an area polluted with sulfur dioxide, there would be fewer lichen species. So lichens are good indicators of pollution.

Study tip

Examples of biological indicators of pollution are lichens for sulfur dioxide and number of invertebrate species for water pollution.

Examples of non-living indicators are oxygen, temperature and pH values.

2 Which indicator species are used to indicate levels of a) air pollution, b) water pollution?

Practical

Indicators of pollution levels

You can investigate both the variety of lichens in your local area and the number of invertebrate species in your local pond or stream. Your data can then be compared to national figures to give you an idea of the pollution levels in your area.

3 What results would you expect if your local area has little air pollution?

Safety: Follow safety advice for outside activities.

⚭ links

Revise more on parasites and their dependence on other organisms in 12.6 'Adaptations in parasites'.

Revise more on factors affecting the distribution of organisms in the environment in 13.1 'Organisms in their environment'.

Student Book
pages 184–185

B13.5 The impact of change

Key points

- Both living and non-living factors can cause changes in the environment.
- Changes in the environment can affect the distribution of living organisms.
- Examples of the effects of environmental changes on the distribution of living organisms include the changes in the distribution of a number of British and European birds and plants in response to rising temperatures, and the fall in the honey bee population as a result of new disease and possible climate change.

Study tip

Use data from any graphs or diagrams, as well as the written information in questions, when describing environmental changes.

- Changes in the environment affect the distribution of living organisms.
- It is sometimes difficult to determine what is affecting the organism.
- Birds may fly further north if the climate gets warmer. Other birds may then have new competitors.
- The large fall in the bee population may have been caused by several factors. These include:
  - the use of chemical sprays by farmers
  - a viral disease
  - changes in the flowering patterns of plants, which may be due to climate change.

1 Why do some birds fly further north to find nesting sites?

2 Give one possible reason for the fall in the bee population.

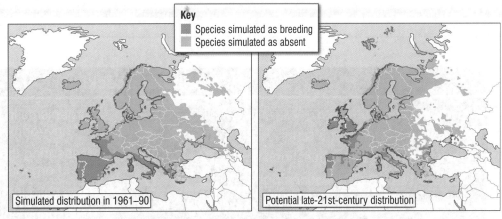

Key
■ Species simulated as breeding
□ Species simulated as absent

Simulated distribution in 1961–90

Potential late-21st-century distribution

Figure 1 The maps show how scientists think the distribution of European bird species might change in the future

1 List three physical factors which affect the distribution of animals.

2 How does cutting down forests affect birds?

3 How can you use a quadrat to make a line transect?

4 What is the difference between a mean and a median?

5 What is meant by 'reproducible results'?

6 Why is it difficult to be sure that an investigation in an outdoor habitat is valid?

7 Name an instrument which can record environmental change over a few weeks.

8 What is the advantage of using lichens instead of an instrument to measure sulfur dioxide pollution?

9 You are asked to monitor the temperature of a greenhouse for two weeks. What are the advantages and disadvantages of using a datalogger with a temperature probe compared with a thermometer?

10 Why is it difficult to interpret data about changes in the distribution of animals and plants?

> **Study tip**
>
> Don't be put off by maths questions in biology exams. The methods are the same! In questions about range, mean, median and mode the numbers used are straightforward, but you do need to learn the terms.

Chapter checklist ✔ ✔ ✔

Tick when you have:

reviewed it after your lesson ☑ ☐ ☐

revised once – some questions right ☑ ☑ ☐

revised twice – all questions right ☑ ☑ ☑

Move on to another topic when you have all three ticks

Organisms in their environment ☐ ☐ ☐

Measuring the distribution of organisms ☐ ☐ ☐

How valid is the data? ☐ ☐ ☐

Measuring environmental change ☐ ☐ ☐

The impact of change ☐ ☐ ☐

B14.1

The effects of the human population explosion

Key points

- The human population is growing rapidly and the standard of living is rising.

- More waste is being produced. If it is not handled properly, it can pollute the water, the air and the land.

- Humans reduce the amount of land available for other animals and plants by building, quarrying, farming and dumping waste.

- There are increasing numbers of people on our planet. Currently the world **population** is about 7 billion!

- Many people want and demand a better standard of living.

- We are using up raw materials, and those that are **non-renewable** cannot be replaced.

- When goods are produced there is a lot of **industrial waste**.

- We are producing more waste and more of the pollution that goes with it.

- Humans reduce the amount of land available for animals and plants by building, quarrying, farming and dumping waste.

- The continuing increase in the human population is affecting the **ecology** of the Earth.

Humans pollute:

- waterways with **sewage**, **fertiliser** and toxic chemicals

- air with smoke and gases such as sulfur dioxide, which contributes to acid rain

- land with toxic chemicals such as pesticides and herbicides and these can then be washed into the water.

▶ **1** *Why does building houses for humans affect animals and plants?*

Study tip

As the human population rapidly increases there is more need for efficient food production. Learn the arguments for and against intensive farming.

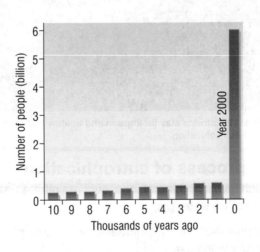
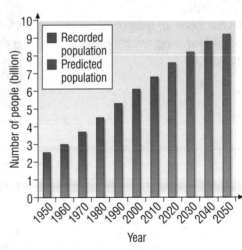

Figure 1 These records of human population growth show the massive increase during the past years. The second bar chart predicts that this increase will continue.

Key words: non-renewable, industrial waste, ecology, sewage, fertiliser

Student Book
pages 190–191 **B14.2**

Land and water pollution

- Sewage contains human body waste and waste water from our homes. Sewage must be treated properly to remove gut parasites and toxic chemicals or these can get on to the land.

- Farming methods can pollute the land.

- Herbicides (weedkillers) and pesticides (which kill insects) are also poisons. The poisons sprayed on to crops can get into the soil and into the food chain. Eventually many of them are washed into rivers and streams.

- Toxic chemicals from landfill also leak into the waterways and pollute the water, killing organisms such as fish.

- Farmers also use chemical fertilisers, to keep the soil **fertile**, which can be washed into rivers.

- Fertilisers and untreated sewage can cause a high level of nitrates in the water which leads to **eutrophication**.

Key points

- Human activities pollute the land and water in several ways.
- Toxic chemicals such as pesticides and herbicides can pollute the land.
- If sewage is not properly handled and treated, it can pollute the water.
- Fertilisers and toxic chemicals can be washed from the land into the water and pollute it.
- Sewage and fertilisers can cause eutrophication in waterways.

Study tip

Learn to describe the sequence of events for eutrophication.

∞ links

Revise more on bioindicators in 13.4 'Measuring environmental change'.

Figure 1 This stream may look green and healthy, but all the animal life it once supported is dead as a result of eutrophication

The process of eutrophication

1 High levels of mineral ions, such as nitrates, stimulate the rapid growth of algae and other water plants.

2 Competition for light increases and many plants die because they cannot photosynthesise.

3 Microorganisms feed on the dead plants so the microorganism population increases rapidly.

4 Respiration by the microorganisms lowers the concentration of oxygen in the water.

5 Most of the aerobic organisms, e.g. fish, die due to a lack of oxygen, so there is even more decay by microorganisms. The lack of oxygen means the water cannot sustain living organisms.

Key words: fertile, eutrophication

▐▐▐➤ **1** *What is the effect of eutrophication on river water?*

B14.3 Air pollution

Key points

- When people burn fossil fuels, carbon dioxide is released into the atmosphere.

- Sulfur dioxide and nitrogen oxides can be released when fossil fuels are burned. These gases dissolve in rainwater and make it more acidic.

- Acid rain may damage trees directly. It can make lakes and rivers too acidic for plants and animals to live in them.

- Air pollution can cause global dimming and smog as tiny solid particles in the air reflect away the sunlight.

- Burning fossil fuels can produce **sulfur dioxide** and other acidic gases.

- By burning **biofuels** instead, these emissions and **smog** can be reduced.

- Power stations and cars release acidic gases.

- The sulfur dioxide dissolves in water in the air, forming acidic solutions.

- The solutions then fall as **acid rain** – sometimes a long way from where the gases were produced.

> 1 *Which gas is the main cause of acid rain?*

- Acid rain kills organisms. Trees can be damaged if the leaves are soaked in acid rain for long periods.

- Acid rain can change the soil pH, which damages roots and may release toxic minerals. For example, aluminium ions are released which also damage organisms in the soil and in waterways.

- Enzymes, which control reactions in organisms, are very sensitive to pH (acidity or alkalinity).

- When trees are damaged, food and habitats for many other organisms are lost.

> 2 *Explain how birds are affected by acid rain.*

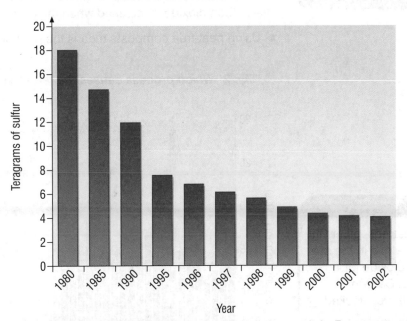

Figure 1 Graph to show the reductions in sulfur emissions made by European countries in recent years

Key words: sulfur dioxide, biofuel, smog, acid rain

Student Book
pages 194–195

B14.4

Deforestation and peat destruction

Deforestation means that many trees are cut down. Large-scale deforestation in tropical areas is due to the need for timber and to provide land for agriculture.

- Deforestation has:
  - increased the release of carbon dioxide into the atmosphere due to burning of the trees or decay of the wood by microorganisms
  - reduced the rate at which carbon dioxide is removed from the atmosphere, by photosynthesis
  - reduced **biodiversity** due to loss of food and habitats.

> **1** *Which process in plants and algae removes carbon dioxide from the air?*

- Deforestation has occurred so that:
  - crops can be grown to produce ethanol and plant oil-based biofuels
  - there can be increases in cattle and rice fields for food.

- Cattle and rice growing produce **methane**, which has led to an increase of methane in the atmosphere.

Peat bogs

- The destruction of peat bogs, and other areas of peat, also results in the release of carbon dioxide into the atmosphere. This occurs because:
  - the peat is removed from the bogs and used in compost for gardens
  - the compost is decayed by microorganisms
  - carbon dioxide is released when the microorganisms respire.

- Using peat-free composts means the peat bogs will not be destroyed.

> **2** *Which process causes the release of carbon dioxide from peat?*

Key points

- Deforestation is the destruction or removal of areas of forest or woodland. Deforestation leads to loss of biodiversity.
- Large-scale deforestation has led to an increase in the amount of carbon dioxide released into the atmosphere (from burning and the actions of microorganisms). It has also reduced the rate at which carbon dioxide is removed from the air by plants.
- More rice fields and cattle have led to increased levels of methane in the atmosphere.
- The destruction of peat bogs releases carbon dioxide into the atmosphere.

Study tip

Remember that trees, plants in peat bogs and algae in the sea all use carbon dioxide for photosynthesis. Carbon compounds are then 'locked up' in these plants.

Try to relate cause and effect. For example, make sure you understand why trees are important. Photosynthesis locks up carbon dioxide in plants. When trees are cut down and burned or decay, the carbon dioxide is released.

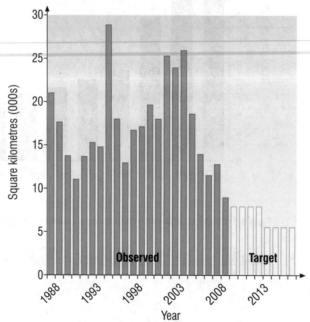

Figure 1 The rate of deforestation is devastating. Even in the high-profile Brazilian Amazon, where deforestation rates are dropping, around 8–10000 km² of tropical rainforest is being lost each year.

Key words: deforestation, biodiversity, methane

Student Book
pages 196–197 **B14.5**

Global warming

- In the normal balance of nature, carbon dioxide is released into the air by respiration and removed by plants and algae in photosynthesis.
- Carbon dioxide also dissolves in oceans, rivers, lakes and ponds.
- We say that the carbon dioxide is **sequestered** (or stored in 'carbon sinks') by plants and water.

> **1 How is carbon dioxide sequestered?**

Levels of carbon dioxide and methane are increasing in the atmosphere. They are called **greenhouse gases** and cause an increased **greenhouse effect**. Most scientists believe an increase in greenhouse gases contributes to **global warming**.

- An increase in the Earth's average temperature of only a few degrees Celsius may:
  - cause big changes in the Earth's climate
  - cause a rise in sea level due to melting of ice caps and glaciers
  - cause changes in migration patterns, e.g. of birds
  - result in changes in the distribution of species
  - reduce biodiversity.

> **2 Why might sea levels rise in the future?**

Key points

- Increasing levels of carbon dioxide and methane in the atmosphere give rise to an increased greenhouse effect, leading to global warming – an increase in the temperature of the surface of the Earth.
- Global warming may cause a number of changes including climate change, a rise in sea level, changes in migration patterns and distribution of species, and loss of biodiversity.
- Global warming will mean that less carbon dioxide is sequestered in oceans and lakes.

∞ links

Revise more on how plants use carbon dioxide to make food in 9.1 'Photosynthesis' and the changes in distribution of organisms in 13.4 'Measuring environmental change'.

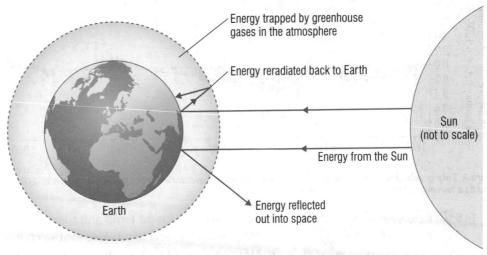

Energy trapped by greenhouse gases in the atmosphere

Energy reradiated back to Earth

Sun (not to scale)

Energy from the Sun

Earth

Energy reflected out into space

Figure 1 The greenhouse effect – vital for life on Earth

Study tip

Remember which gas is which!

Increased levels of carbon dioxide and methane enhance the greenhouse effect, which causes global warming.

Sulfur dioxide and nitrogen oxides cause acid rain.

Key words: sequestered, greenhouse gas, greenhouse effect, global warming

Student Book
pages 198–199 **B14.6** # Analysing the evidence

- There are huge amounts of environmental data produced by many different scientists in many different countries. It can be difficult to be sure that the data are valid, reproducible and repeatable.
- Scientists often come to different conclusions even when considering the same data. Explanations sometimes depend on the individual opinions of the scientist and can be biased.
- The issue of global warming divides opinion. Many people think the Earth's temperature has increased due to increases in greenhouse gases. Others say the increase is part of a natural cycle.
- In an attempt to collect valid, reproducible and repeatable data, scientists measure a range of factors such as daily temperature, carbon dioxide levels, weather patterns and distribution of living organisms.

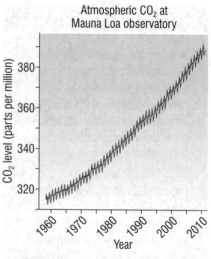

Figure 1 The atmospheric carbon dioxide readings for this graph are taken monthly on a mountain top in Hawaii. There is a clear upward trend, which shows no sign of slowing down.

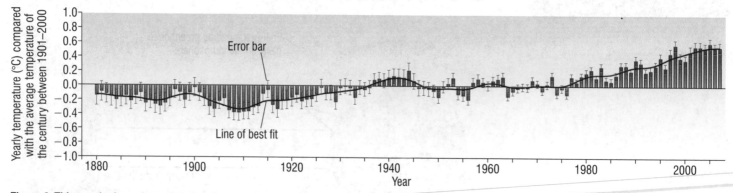

Figure 2 This graph shows how global surface temperatures have varied from the mean for 1901–2000 over 130 years. These data are widely regarded as very repeatable and reproducible.

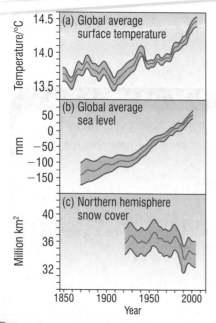

Figure 3 These graphs, published by the IPCC (Intergovernmental Panel on Climate Change) show what seems to be a clear correlation between rising temperatures, melting snow and rising sea levels

- Scientists look for patterns and trends in the data collected but often they cannot make a definite link to a cause for the changes.
- Most scientists believe there is a link between human activities and some of the changes seen in the climate, but how much humans have affected the normal cycle of climate changes is still causing some debate.

1 Why is it difficult to prove that human activities have caused climate change?

2 Look at the graph of global surface temperature. Describe the pattern.

1 What are herbicides?

2 Sulfur dioxide is the main gas that causes acid rain. Name another acid gas that can contribute to acid rain.

3 Why does acid rain often fall a great distance from where it was produced?

4 How is methane produced?

5 When trees are cut down, carbon dioxide is released into the atmosphere. Explain how.

6 Name three pollutants which can move from land into rivers and streams.

7 Why does deforestation cause a reduction in biodiversity?

8 Why are gardeners encouraged to buy peat-free compost?

9 Describe the sequence of events in eutrophication.

10 Why do most scientists think that human activities are causing global warming and climate change?

> **Study tip**
>
> Look for examples in the media of how humans pollute the Earth and for ways of controlling pollution.

Chapter checklist

Tick when you have:

reviewed it after your lesson ☑ ☐ ☐

revised once – some questions right ☑ ☑ ☐

revised twice – all questions right ☑ ☑ ☑

Move on to another topic when you have all three ticks

The effects of the human population explosion ☐ ☐ ☐

Land and water pollution ☐ ☐ ☐

Air pollution ☐ ☐ ☐

Deforestation and peat destruction ☐ ☐ ☐

Global warming ☐ ☐ ☐

Analysing the evidence ☐ ☐ ☐

Student Book
pages 202–203

B15.1 Theories of evolution

Key points

- The theory of evolution states that all the species that are alive today – and many more which are now extinct – evolved from simple life forms that first developed more than 3 billion years ago.

- Darwin's theory is that evolution takes place through natural selection.

- The evidence for Darwin's theory came from his observations while on a scientific expedition to the Galapagos Islands in the 1830s.

- Darwin discovered that variations between species of finches, iguanas and tortoises reflected how each species had adapted and evolved to suit life on a different island.

Key words: evolution, Jean-Baptiste Lamarck, inheritance of acquired characteristics, Charles Darwin, natural selection

- Scientists have estimated that life began on Earth about 3 billion years ago.
- Before the 18th century there were few scientific ideas about how **evolution** works.
- **Jean-Baptiste Lamarck** suggested a theory called 'the **inheritance of acquired characteristics**'. Lamarck's theory stated that characteristics which develop during an organism's lifetime can be passed on to the next generation. People found this difficult to believe. For example, if two parents were to build up their muscles in the gym, Lamarck's theory would predict that this characteristic would be passed on to their offspring.

> **1** *What is meant by acquired characteristics?*

- **Charles Darwin** suggested the theory of '**natural selection**' after he had made a journey to the Galapagos Islands. He recorded many observations about wildlife on the islands.
- Darwin's theory stated that small changes in organisms took place over a very long time. All organisms in a species vary and therefore some are more likely to survive (natural selection). Those that are best adapted breed and pass on their characteristics.
- Darwin did not know about genes. We can now say that the best adapted organisms survive to breed. They are the ones that pass on their genes to the next generation.

> **2** *Who suggested the theory of evolution by natural selection?*

Study tip

Remember the key steps in natural selection:
Mutation of gene → advantage to survival → breed → pass on genes.

Student Book
pages 204–205

B15.2 Accepting Darwin's ideas

Key points

- Darwin's theory of evolution by natural selection was only gradually accepted for a number of reasons. These include:
  – a conflict with the widely held belief that God made all the animals and plants on the Earth
  – insufficient evidence
  – no mechanism for explaining variety and inheritance (genetics were not understood for another 50 years).

Darwin's theory of evolution by natural selection was only gradually accepted for several reasons:

- The theory of natural selection challenged the idea that God made all the animals and plants that live on Earth.
- Many scientists were not convinced because they still did not think there was sufficient evidence for the theory.

> **1** *What name is given to Darwin's theory of evolution?*

- Darwin could not explain why there was variety in organisms, or how inheritance worked. Scientists did not know about genes and genetics until about 50 years later.
- Darwin had tried to show that birds, such as finches on the Galapagos Islands, could change over time if they lived under different environmental conditions. During his lifetime he could not explain, in terms of genes, how the offspring inherited the useful adaptations.

> **2** *Which birds did Darwin observe to find evidence for evolution?*

B15.3 **Natural selection**

Key points

- Natural selection works by selecting the organisms best adapted to a particular environment.

- Different organisms in a species may show a wide range of variation because of differences in their genes.

- The individuals with the characteristics most suited to their environment are most likely to survive and breed successfully.

- The genes that have produced these successful characteristics are then passed on to the next generation.

- The timescales of evolution vary depending on the complexity and life cycle of organisms; for example, simple organisms such as bacteria evolve much faster than complex multicellular organisms such as mammals.

∞ links

Revise more on the competition between plants and animals in the natural world in 12.4 'Competition in animals' and 12.5 'Competition in plants'.

Revise more on genes in 10.1 'Inheritance' and the evolution of antibiotic-resistant bacteria by natural selection in 8.5 'Changing pathogens'.

Revise more on evolutionary timescales in 15.7 'More about extinction'.

- Most organisms produce large numbers of offspring. For example, a pair of rabbits may have 800 children, grandchildren and great grandchildren in one nine-month breeding season!

- Individual organisms will show a wide range of variation because of differences in their genes.

- All the organisms in the population will compete for food, shelter from predators, and mates.

- The organisms with the characteristics most suited to the environment will survive. For example, the best camouflage, the best eyesight to find food, the strongest to build a burrow, the quickest to run from a predator, the best suited to the climate. The 'fittest' organisms survive.

▐▶ **1 Why do organisms show a wide range of variation?**

- The organisms which survive are more likely to breed successfully.

- The genes that have enabled these organisms to survive are then passed on to their offspring.

- Sometimes a gene accidentally changes and becomes a new form of the gene. These changes are called **mutations**. If the mutated gene controls a characteristic which makes the organism better adapted to the environment, then it will be passed on to the offspring.

- Mutations may be particularly important in natural selection if the environment changes. For example, when the rabbit disease myxomatosis killed most of the rabbits in the UK, a few rabbits had a mutated gene that gave them immunity. The rabbits with the mutated gene survived to breed.

- Evolution of a new species can take millions of years but sometimes evolution of a population occurs in a relatively short time. For example, if a bacterium has a mutation that makes it resistant to antibiotics, then this mutation can spread rapidly through the population until all the bacteria are resistant.

▐▶ **2 Why did some rabbits survive myxomatosis?**

Figure 1 The natural world is often brutal. Only the best-adapted predators capture prey and survive to breed – and only the best-adapted prey animals escape to breed as well.

Study tip

When answering questions on evolution, use the following terms accurately and in the best sequence: mutation → variation → best adapted → survival → breed → genes passed on to offspring.

B15.4 Classification and evolution

Key points

- Studying the similarities and differences between organisms allows us to classify them into animals, plants and microorganisms.
- Classification also helps us to understand evolutionary and ecological relationships.
- Models such as evolutionary trees allow us to suggest relationships between organisms.

Study tip

Remember, a species is a group of organisms that can successfully breed together to produce fertile offspring.

- There are millions of different types of living organisms. By putting organisms into groups we can make more sense of how closely they are related. Grouping organisms is called **classification**.
- Biologists study the similarities and differences between organisms in order to classify them. The system used is called the **natural classification system**.
- The easiest system to understand is one which starts with large groups and splits these up gradually into smaller ones. The largest groups are called **kingdoms**.
- The main kingdoms are:
  - the plant kingdom
  - the animal kingdom
  - the kingdoms which contain the microorganisms.
- The smallest group in the classification system is the **species**.
- Members of a species are very similar and can breed together to produce fertile offspring.

➡ **1** *What are the main kingdoms of living organisms?*

- **Evolutionary trees** are models that can be drawn to show the relationships between different groups of organisms.
- When new evidence is found, biologists may modify these **evolutionary relationships**.
- Ecological relationships tell us how species have evolved together in an environment.

➡ **2** *Why is it useful to draw evolutionary trees?*

Study tip

Remember the difference:
- natural selection is a process taking many generations
- evolution is the theory of how species changed over millions of years.

So evolution takes place over a much longer timescale than natural selection.

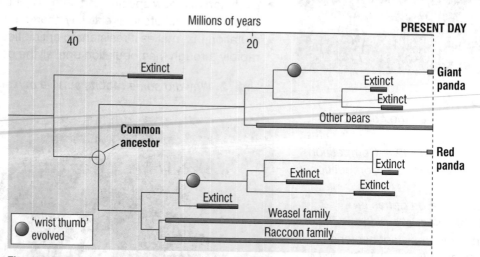

Figure 1 Evolutionary trees like this show us the best model of the evolutionary relationships between organisms

Key words: classification, natural classification system, kingdom, species, evolutionary tree, evolutionary relationship

B15.5   # The origins of life on Earth

Key points

- Fossils are the remains of organisms from millions of years ago that are found in rocks.

- Fossils may be formed in different ways.

- Fossils give us information about organisms that lived millions of years ago.

- It is very difficult for scientists to know exactly how life on Earth began because there is little evidence that is valid.

- It is believed that the Earth is about 4.5 billion years old, and that life began about 3.5 billion years ago.

- There is some debate about whether the first life developed due to the conditions on Earth, or whether simple life forms arrived from another planet.

- We can date rocks. **Fossils** are found in rocks, so we can date when different organisms existed.

- Fossils may be formed in various ways:
  - from the hard parts of animals that do not decay easily, e.g. bones, teeth, shells, claws
  - from parts of organisms that have not decayed because some of the conditions for decay are absent, e.g. fossils of animals preserved in ice
  - when parts of the organism are replaced by other materials, such as minerals, as they decay
  - as preserved traces of organisms, e.g. footprints, burrows and rootlet traces.

- Most organisms that died did not leave a fossil because the exact conditions for fossil formation were not present.

> **1** *Name a hard part of an animal that will not decay easily.*

- Many early life forms had soft bodies so few traces were left behind.
- Traces which were left are likely to have been destroyed by geological activity such as earthquakes.

> **2** *Why is the fossil record incomplete?*

Figure 1 Trilobites lived from between 525 and 250 million years ago, but some of the fossils are so good they still look almost alive

 Maths skills

The timescales involved in the development of life on Earth are huge.
4500 million years is the same as 4.5 billion years or 4 500 000 000.
To save writing a whole string of zeros, it is easier to write 4.5×10^9.
Try to remember a thousand is 10^3, a million is 10^6 and a billion is 10^9.

Key word: fossil

B15.6 Exploring the fossil evidence

Student Book
pages 212–213

Key points

- We can learn from fossils how much or how little organisms have changed as life has developed on Earth.
- Extinction may be caused by a number of factors including new predators, new diseases or new, more successful competitors.

Study tip

Always mention a *change* when you give possible reasons for the extinction of a species.

links

Revise more on fossil records in 15.5 'The origins of life on Earth' and the role of environmental changes and catastrophic events in evolution in 15.7 'More about extinction'.

- The fossil record is incomplete, but we can learn a lot from the fossils which do exist. Some organisms have changed a lot over time. Others have changed very little, while some have become extinct.
- **Extinction** means that a species which once existed has completely died out.

Extinction can be caused by a number of factors, but always involves a change in circumstances:

- A new disease may kill all members of a species.
- The environment changes over geological time.
- New diseases may be introduced.
- A new predator may evolve or be introduced to an area that effectively kills and eats all of a species.
- A new competitor may evolve or be introduced into an area. The original species may be left with too little to eat.
- A single catastrophic event may occur which destroys the habitat, e.g. a massive volcanic eruption.
- Natural changes in species occur over time.

⮞ **1** *How can a new predator cause extinction of a species?*

⮞ **2** *Name a catastrophic event that could destroy a large number of habitats.*

Key word: extinction

B15.7 More about extinction

Student Book
pages 214–215

Key points

- Extinction can be caused by environmental change over geological time.
- Mass extinctions may be caused by single catastrophic events, such as volcanoes or asteroid strikes, which cause a sudden and dramatic change in the environment.

Study tip

Remember that the timescales in forming new species and mass extinctions are huge.
Try to develop an understanding of time in millions and billions of years.

- The biggest influences on the survival of species are changes in the environment.
- Climate change is an important influence in determining which species survive. A species which is very well adapted to a hot climate may become extinct in an Ice Age. It could be that there is insufficient food or it is too cold to breed.
- Climate change may make it too cold or hot, or wet or dry, for a species and reduce its food supply.

⮞ **1** *Why might a species die out if the climate changes?*

- Fossil evidence shows that there have been mass extinctions on a global scale. Many of the species died out over a period of several million years – a short time in geological terms.
  - The habitat the species lives in may be destroyed by catastrophic events such as a major volcanic eruption.
  - The environment can change dramatically following a collision between a giant asteroid and Earth.
- Why the dinosaurs became extinct has puzzled many scientists. Different ideas have been suggested. For example:
  - the collision of a giant asteroid caused huge fires, earthquakes, landslides and tsunamis. The dust which rose masked the Sun causing darkness and lower temperatures. Plants could not grow and temperatures fell.
  - the extinction was a slower process due to sea ice melting and cooling the sea temperature by about 9 °C, therefore there was less plankton – less food available.

⮞ **2** *Suggest another factor which could have caused the dinosaurs to die out.*

B15.8 Isolation and the evolution of new species

Key points

- New species arise as a result of:
  - Isolation: two populations of a species become separated, e.g. geographically.
  - Genetic variation: each population has a wide range of alleles that control their characteristics.
  - Natural selection: in each population the alleles are selected that control the characteristics which help the organism to survive and breed.
  - Speciation: the populations become so different that successful interbreeding is no longer possible.

links

Revise more on genetic variation and natural selection in 15.3 'Natural selection'.

Study tip

To bump up your grade, make sure you understand the process of speciation. Write logically using the correct terms: isolation → genetic variation → alleles selected → interbreeding no longer possible → new species (speciation).

Speciation is a difficult concept. If you cannot remember all the steps, at least remember that: two groups of the same species became separated and different natural selection takes place in each group, so eventually they become so different that they are no longer able to breed.

- New species can arise from existing species if a group becomes isolated from the rest.
- **Geographical isolation** could occur if an island separates from the mainland or if a new river separates two areas. Mountain ranges and old craters can isolate organisms.
- The organisms left on the island may be exposed to different environmental conditions. If the environment, competitors, food supply and predators are different for each population, they will evolve differently.
- Each population has a wide range of alleles that control their characteristics. This is genetic variation. Natural selection will occur in both areas, but different characteristics will be beneficial in the two populations. The alleles that control the characteristics which help the organism to survive are selected. The organisms with these alleles will survive and breed.
- If the populations are brought together and cannot interbreed, we say that they belong to two separate species and **speciation** has occurred.
- When a species evolves in isolation and is found in only one place in the world it is said to be **endemic** (particular) to that area.

▶ **1** *How do populations become isolated?*

▶ **2** *What is meant by 'genetic variation'?*

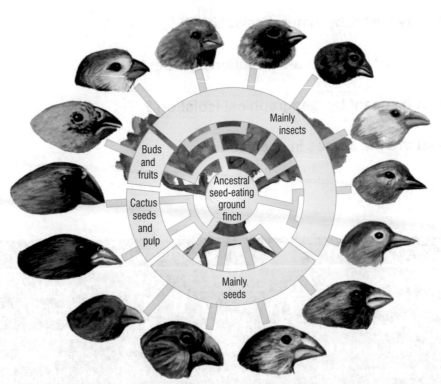

Figure 1 Darwin's finches became isolated on different islands. The conditions, particularly the type of food present, varied on each island. The finches developed differently due to the alleles which were selected in natural selection.

Key words: geographical isolation, speciation, endemic

1 **a** What is the approximate age of the Earth?

   b When do we think life on Earth began?

2 Why are there no fossils of early life forms?

3 How would you write three billion in standard form?

4 How might a new competitor cause the extinction of a species?

5 What are the two main ideas put forward for the extinction of dinosaurs?

6 Suggest three factors that could change in a habitat area, causing problems for the organisms living there.

7 What is the main difference between Lamarck's theory of evolution and Darwin's theory?

8 Why is there variation between members of the same species?

9 What is meant by 'natural selection'?

10 Why do biologists draw evolutionary trees?

11 What is meant by 'geographical isolation'?

12 What are the stages in speciation?

Study tip

Remember that no one knows exactly why the dinosaurs became extinct. There were no scientists around at the time! Ideas suggested are based on the evidence we have. If new evidence is found, such as clues from newly discovered fossils, the ideas could change.

Always mention a change when referring to extinction. If things stay the same, the species will continue to live successfully in its habitat.

Chapter checklist

Tick when you have:

reviewed it after your lesson ☑ ☐ ☐

revised once – some questions right ☑ ☑ ☐

revised twice – all questions right ☑ ☑ ☑

Move on to another topic when you have all three ticks

Theories of evolution	☐	☐	☐
Accepting Darwin's ideas	☐	☐	☐
Natural selection	☐	☐	☐
Classification and evolution	☐	☐	☐
The origins of life on Earth	☐	☐	☐
Exploring the fossil evidence	☐	☐	☐
More about extinction	☐	☐	☐
Isolation and the evolution of new species	☐	☐	☐

**Student Book
pages 220–221**

B16.1 Pyramids of biomass

Key points

- Radiation from the Sun is the main source of energy for all living things. The Sun's light energy is captured by green plants and algae during photosynthesis, and transferred to chemical energy, which is stored in the substances that make up the cells. This is new biomass.

- Biomass is the mass of living material in an animal or plant. We can measure dry biomass or wet biomass.

- At each stage of a food chain, biomass is less than at the previous stage because some is lost in the waste materials of the organism and some is used for living processes such as movement.

- The biomass at each stage can be drawn to scale and shown as a pyramid of biomass.

- **Biomass** is the mass of living material in plants and animals.

- A **pyramid of biomass** represents the mass of the organisms at each stage in a food chain. It may be more accurate than a pyramid of numbers. For example, one bush may have many insects feeding on it but the mass of the bush is far greater than the mass of the insects.

- Green plants transfer **solar (light) energy** to chemical energy which is then passed through the food chain.

> **1** Why are plants always at the base of the pyramid of biomass?

> **2** What is the source of energy for pyramids of biomass?

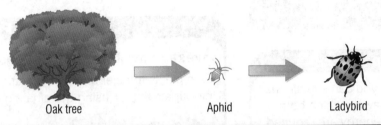

| Oak tree | Aphid | Ladybird |

Organism	Number	Biomass – dry mass in g
Oak tree	1	500 000
Aphids	10 000	1000
Ladybirds	200	50

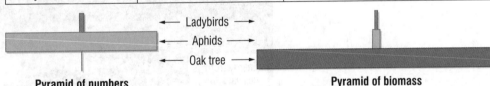

← Ladybirds →
← Aphids →
← Oak tree →

Pyramid of numbers   **Pyramid of biomass**

Figure 1 Using a pyramid of biomass shows us the amount of biological material involved at each level of this food chain much more effectively than using a pyramid of numbers

Study tip

Examiners always try to present information in new ways. To gain marks from data, which may be given as tables, graphs, charts, unusual diagrams as well as in writing, read the introduction to the question carefully, and check you know what information is given on all the illustrations. If you have not used the data in your answer, you may have missed the point of the question.

Key words: biomass, pyramid of biomass, solar (light) energy

Student Book
pages 222–223

B16.2

Energy transfers

- There is energy wastage between each stage of a food chain. So not all the energy taken in by an organism results in the growth of that organism.
- Not all the food that is eaten can be digested, so energy is stored in faeces or as urea in urine (waste materials).
- Some biomass (food) is used for respiration, which releases energy for living processes, including movement. The more an organism moves, the more energy it uses and so less is available for growth.
- For animals whose bodies are normally at a constant temperature, some energy is used from the previous stage of the food chain to achieve this.
- Much of the energy released in respiration is eventually transferred to the surroundings.

⟹ **1** *Which process in cells releases energy from food material?*

Key points

- The amounts of biomass and energy get less at each successive stage in a food chain.
- This is because some material and energy are always lost in waste materials, and some are used for respiration to supply energy for living processes, including movement. Much of the energy is eventually transferred to the surroundings as heat.

Study tip

Make sure you can explain the different ways in which both mass and energy are reduced between the stages of a food chain.

Practical

Investigating the energy released by respiration

Even plants transfer energy by heating their surroundings in respiration. You can investigate this by using germinating peas in a vacuum flask.

⟹ **2** *What would be the best way to monitor the temperature continuously?*

Figure 1 Only between 2% and 10% of the biomass eaten by an animal such as this horse will get turned into new horse. The rest of the stored energy will be used for movement or transferred, heating the surroundings, or lost in waste materials.

Student Book
pages 224–225

B16.3 Making food production efficient

Key points

- Biomass and energy are reduced at each stage of a food chain. The efficiency of food production is improved by reducing the number of stages in a food chain.
- The efficiency of food production can also be improved by restricting energy loss from animals by limiting their movement and by controlling the temperature of their surroundings.

∞ links

Revise more on pyramids of biomass in 16.1 'Pyramids of biomass' and energy losses though a food chain in 16.2 'Energy transfers'.

- The shorter the food chain, the less energy will be wasted. It is therefore more efficient for us to eat plants than it is to eat animals.
- We can produce meat more efficiently by:
  - preventing the animal from moving so it doesn't waste energy on movement; but this is seen as cruel by many people and is controversial
  - keeping the animal in warm sheds so it doesn't use as much energy from food to maintain its body temperature.
- Efficiency of food production also depends on how far the food is transported before we buy it. Eating locally grown food reduces the number of 'food miles' so that fuel consumption is decreased.

> 1 *Animals are sometimes kept in warm sheds. Explain why.*
>
> 2 *Suggest what is meant by 'food miles'.*

Study tip

Be clear about the ways in which the efficiency of food production can be improved to meet the needs of a growing human population. Make sure you have considered the advantages and disadvantages of each method before your examination.

Student Book
pages 226–227

B16.4 Sustainable food production

Key points

- Sustainable food production means producing food in a way which can continue for many years.
- It is important to control the size of nets used and impose fishing quotas to conserve fish stocks, so breeding continues and the decline in numbers is halted.
- New foods can be developed with reduced stages in the food chain for efficient production.

Study tip

Learn what can be done to conserve fish stocks so that we will have fish in the future.

Key words: sustainable food production, mycoprotein

The human population is increasing rapidly and food resources are at risk of running out.

Sustainable food production involves managing resources, and finding new types of food such as **mycoprotein**. This ensures there is enough food for the current population and in the future.

- Fish stocks in the oceans are declining.
- To maintain fish stocks, fishermen:
  - can only remove a strict allocation of fish (a quota) per year so the numbers of fishing trips are reduced
  - must use nets with a mesh large enough to avoid catching small, young fish so they can grow to full size and breed.
- If these measures are not implemented, some species of fish could become extinct.

> 1 *Why aren't fishermen allowed to remove small, young fish?*

- The fungus *Fusarium* is grown to produce mycoprotein. This is a protein-rich food suitable for vegetarians. *Fusarium* is grown aerobically on cheap sugar syrup made from waste starch and the mycoprotein harvested. Developing foods such as mycoprotein could help to solve the problem of world food shortages.

> 2 *What is grown to produce mycoprotein?*

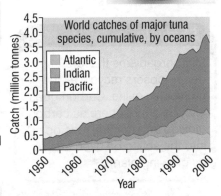

Figure 1 Tuna catches have increased enormously over time to the point where some species are almost extinct

B16.5 # Decay processes

Key points

- Living things remove materials from the environment as they grow. They return them when they die through the action of the decomposers.

- Materials decay because they are broken down (digested) by microorganisms. Microorganisms digest materials faster in warm, moist conditions. Many of them also need oxygen.

- The decay process releases substances that plants need to grow.

- In a stable community, the processes that remove materials (particularly plant growth) are balanced by the processes that return materials, so the materials are part of a constant cycle.

- All organisms take up nutrients. If they didn't eventually release them, the nutrients would run out.

- **Detritus feeders** or **detritivores** (such as some types of worm) may start the process of decay by eating dead animals or plants and producing waste materials. Decay organisms then break down the waste or dead plants and animals.

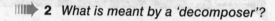 **1** *Give an example of a detritus feeder.*

- Decay organisms are microorganisms (bacteria and fungi). They are called **decomposers**. Decay is faster if it is warm and wet. Many decomposers also need oxygen.

- All of the materials from the waste and dead organisms are recycled, returning nutrients to the soil.

- Humans can recycle waste in **sewage treatment plants** and **compost heaps**.

2 *What is meant by a 'decomposer'?*

Figure 1 This orange is slowly being broken down by the action of decomposers. You can see the fungi clearly but the bacteria are too small to be seen.

Practical

Investigating decay

You can investigate the effect of temperature on how quickly things decay.

 3 *Suggest how you could measure the rate of decay at each temperature chosen in the investigation.*

Study tip

Microorganisms that are decomposers recycle all the molecules of life. Carbon goes into the atmosphere as carbon dioxide and mineral ions go into the soil to be used again by growing plants.

Key words: detritus feeder, detritivore, decomposer, sewage treatment plant, compost heap

Student Book
pages 230–231

B16.6 The carbon cycle

Key points

- The constant cycling of carbon in nature is called the carbon cycle.
- Carbon dioxide is removed from the atmosphere by photosynthesis in plants and algae. It is returned to the atmosphere through respiration of all living organisms including the decomposers, and through combustion of wood and fossil fuels.

- The **carbon cycle** involves both photosynthesis and respiration.
- Photosynthesis removes CO_2 from the atmosphere. The CO_2 and other **elements** are used to make organic **molecules** (carbohydrates, fats and proteins).
- Green plants and algae as well as animals respire. This returns CO_2 to the atmosphere.
- When humans cut down trees less CO_2 is absorbed for photosynthesis. Burning the trees (**combustion**) releases CO_2 into the atmosphere.
- Animals eat green plants and build the carbon into their bodies.
- **Detritus feeders** are animals such as worms which feed on waste or dead bodies of organisms.
- When plants, algae or animals die (or produce waste), microorganisms release the CO_2 back into the atmosphere through respiration. Mineral nutrients return to the soil.
- Combustion of wood and **fossil fuels** releases CO_2 from **carbon sinks** into the atmosphere.
- A stable community recycles all of the nutrients it takes up.

1 *Which process takes carbon dioxide out of the atmosphere?*

2 *What is meant by a 'carbon sink'?*

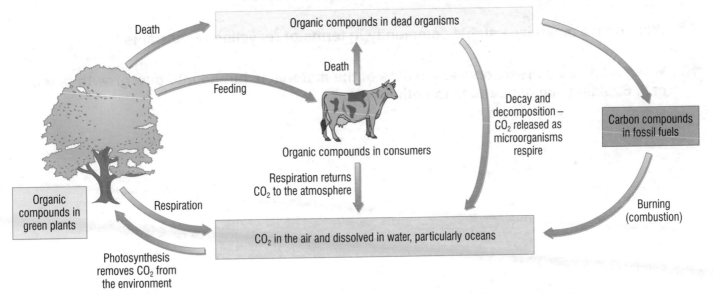

Figure 1 The carbon cycle in nature. Organic compounds include carbohydrates, fats and proteins which all contain carbon.

Study tip

Make sure you can label the processes in a diagram of the carbon cycle.

Key words: carbon cycle, element, molecule, combustion, detritus feeder, fossil fuel, carbon sink

1 What does the word 'biomass' mean?

2 What are organic compounds? Give one example.

3 Which processes return carbon dioxide into the atmosphere?

4 How can energy wastage be reduced in a food chain?

5 Give an example of a detritus feeder.

6 What type of organism is usually at the bottom of a pyramid of biomass?

7 Humans throw waste garden material into a compost heap. The heap gets hot. Explain why.

8 Why do we normally eat herbivores rather than carnivores?

9 What do we mean by a stable community in terms of recycling of nutrients?

10 When a calf eats grass, only about 30% of the material is turned into new growth of the calf. Explain what happens to the other 70%.

Study tip

To improve your grade, check that you understand what is happening to the biomass through a food chain. Energy is never 'lost', it is transferred. Not all the energy which is transferred to the next stage is converted into growth. The energy may heat the surroundings or be stored in faeces.

Chapter checklist

Tick when you have:

reviewed it after your lesson	✓	☐	☐
revised once – some questions right	✓	✓	☐
revised twice – all questions right	✓	✓	✓

Move on to another topic when you have all three ticks

Pyramids of biomass	☐	☐	☐
Energy transfers	☐	☐	☐
Making food production efficient	☐	☐	☐
Sustainable food production	☐	☐	☐
Decay processes	☐	☐	☐
The carbon cycle	☐	☐	☐

1 a i Calculate the surface area to volume ratio for the two cubes A and B.

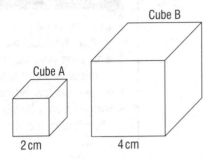

Cube B

Cube A

2 cm   4 cm   *(4 marks)*

ii Some organisms have the same volume as Cube B but a much larger surface area. How is the body shape of these organisms adapted to increase the surface area?   *(1 mark)*

b Scientists have been monitoring populations of organisms in the Antarctic. The water is getting warmer due to climate change.

Scientists observed that the smaller organisms in some populations survive better than larger organisms. In terms of surface area to volume ratio, explain why.   *(2 marks)*

c As the water gets warmer, less oxygen is dissolved in it. This affects the growth of the organisms. Explain why.   *(2 marks)*

d The increasing temperature of the Antarctic could affect the evolution of a population of fish. Explain how.   *(4 marks)*

2 Copper compounds are found in water that has drained through ash from power stations. Invertebrate animals are used to monitor the concentration of copper compounds in water. First, scientists must find out which invertebrate animals can survive in a range of concentrations of copper compounds.

This is how the procedure is carried out:

Solutions of different concentrations of a copper compound are prepared.

Batches of 50 of each of five different invertebrate species, **A**, **B**, **C**, **D** and **E**, are placed in separate containers of each solution.

After a while, the number of each type of invertebrate which survive at each concentration is counted.

a Give **two** variables that should be controlled in this investigation so that the results are valid.   *(2 marks)*

b The graph shows the results for species B.

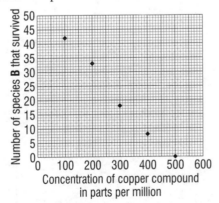

Use the graph to find the concentration of copper compounds (in parts per million) in which 50% of species **B** survived. To obtain full marks you must show clearly on a copy of the graph how you obtained your answer.   *(2 marks)*

c The graph shows the results of the tests on the other four invertebrate species.

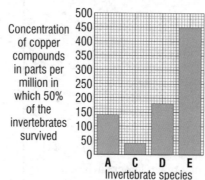

i Which species, **A**, **C**, **D** or **E**, is most sensitive to the concentration of copper in the water? Give the reason for your answer. *(1 mark)*

ii It is often more convenient to use invertebrates rather than a chemical test to monitor water for copper. Suggest **two** explanations for this. *(2 marks)*

Student Book
pages 234–242

Investigations

Key points

- Plan investigations to produce repeatable, reproducible and valid results. Take care to ensure fair testing.

- Careful use of the correct equipment can improve accuracy. The mean of a repeat set of readings is the sum of the values divided by how many values there are.

- Human error can produce random and systematic errors. Examine anomalous results and discard them if necessary.

- The reproducibility of data can be checked by looking at similar work done by others, by using a different method or by others checking your method.

Study tip

Trial runs will tell you a lot about how your investigation might work out. They should get you to ask yourself:
- Do you have the correct conditions?
- Have you chosen a sensible range?
- Have you got readings that are close together?
- Will you need to repeat your readings?

Study tip

When you draw a results table, put the independent variable in the first column, and the dependent variable in the other column(s). When you draw a graph, plot the independent variable along the horizontal axis and the dependent variable up the vertical axis.

Key words: reproducible, repeatable, valid

Investigations

- The **independent variable** is the one you choose to vary in your investigation.
- The **dependent variable** is used to judge the effect of varying the independent variable.
- A fair test is one in which only the independent variable affects the dependent variable. All other variables are controlled and kept constant if at all possible. (In fieldwork, the best you can do is to make sure that each of the many control variables change in much the same way.)
- If you are investigating two variables in a large population then you will need to do a survey. Again, it is impossible to control all the variables. So here, the larger the sample size tested, the more valid the results will be.
- Variables can be one of two different types:
  - A **categoric variable** is one that is best described by a label (usually a word). Eye colour is a categoric variable, e.g. blue or brown.
  - A **continuous variable** is one that we measure, so its value could be any number.
- When you are designing an investigation you must make sure that others can repeat any results you get – this makes it **reproducible**. You should also plan to make each result **repeatable**. You can do this by getting consistent sets of repeat measurements.
- You must also make sure you are measuring the actual thing you want to measure. You need to make sure that you have controlled as many other variables as you can, so that no one can say that your investigation is not **valid**.
- A precise set of repeat readings is grouped closely together.
- An accurate set of measurements will have a mean (average) close to the true value.

Setting up investigations

- Even when an instrument is used correctly, the results can still show differences. Results may differ because of a random error. This could be due to poor measurements being made. It could be due to not carrying out the method consistently. The error may be a systematic error. This means that the method was carried out consistently but an error was being repeated.
- Anomalous results are clearly out of line with the rest of the data collected. If they are simply due to a random error then they should be ignored. If anomalies can be identified while you are doing an investigation, then it is best to repeat that part of the investigation. If you find anomalies after you have finished collecting the data for an investigation (perhaps when drawing your graph), then they should be discarded.

Using data

- If you have a categoric independent variable and a continuous dependent variable then you should use a bar chart to display your data.
- If you have a continuous independent and a continuous dependent variable then use a line graph.
- If you are still uncertain about a conclusion, you could check reproducibility by:
  - looking for other similar work on the internet or from others in your class
  - getting somebody else to redo your investigation
  - trying an alternative method to see if you get the same results.
- You will find Paper 2-style questions designed to test your understanding of practical skills included in the pages of Practice questions in this Revision Guide.

Some students wanted to find out if germinating peas respire.

The teacher provided the students with some dried peas that had been soaked in water for one day. Dried peas are inactive but soaked peas become active again.

The students used the soaked peas to set up the apparatus shown. When the pump is turned on air is sucked through the apparatus.

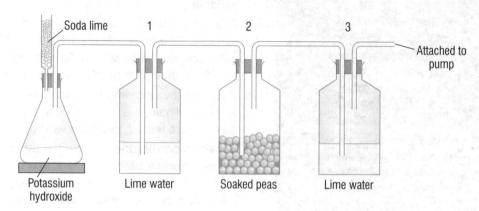

Soda lime | 1 | 2 | 3 | Attached to pump

Potassium hydroxide | Lime water | Soaked peas | Lime water

Remember that answers to questions asking you to 'explain why' should always contain 'because' or 'so'.
In question (a)(i), the answer would gain 2 out of 3 marks as the 'because' statement is missing.

1 (a) **(i)** Soda lime and potassium hydroxide absorb carbon dioxide. Explain why these chemicals are necessary in this investigation.

Air contains carbon dioxide which must be removed.

(3)

Always be precise with answers. A better student would say that the lime water turned cloudy or milky.

1 (a) **(ii)** What is the purpose of the lime water in flask 1?

It checks to see if there is no carbon dioxide left.

(1)

1 (a) **(iii)** If the peas respire, what will happen to the lime water in flask 3?

The lime water will change colour.

(1)

Many students think temperature is an important control in all experiments. Better students read all of the information. In question a iv, you need to be clear about '**the** control' and 'controlling variables'. Here, the control is 'use dried peas instead of soaked peas'.

1 (a) **(iv)** Describe a suitable control for this experiment.

Make sure the temperature stays the same.

(1)

1 (b) Explain why pea seeds are used in this experiment rather than cress seedlings.

The cress would photosynthesise.

(2)

In question (b), the 'so' statement is missing and therefore the student loses a mark.

Mark scheme

a **i** Air contains carbon dioxide (1) which must be removed (1) because they want to find out if carbon dioxide is produced in respiration (1).

ii To check that there is no carbon dioxide left (before air goes into flask 2) (1)

iii The lime water will turn cloudy/milky (1)

iv Put dry peas in flask 2 (1)

b The cress would also photosynthesise (1) so the carbon dioxide would be used/only oxygen would be released. (1)

(8)

Glossary

Abdomen: The lower region of the body. In humans it contains the digestive organs, kidneys, etc.

Acid rain: Rain that is acidic due to dissolved gases, such as sulphur dioxide, produced by the burning of fossil fuels.

Active site: The site on an enzyme where the reactants bind.

Active transport: The movement of substances against a concentration gradient and/or across a cell membrane, using energy.

Adaptation: Special feature that makes an organism particularly well suited to the environment where it lives.

ADH: Anti-diuretic hormone secreted by the pituitary gland in the brain that affects the amount of water lost through the kidneys in the urine.

Adult cell cloning: Process in which the nucleus of an adult cell of one animal is fused with an empty egg from another animal. The embryo which results is placed inside the uterus of a third animal to develop.

Adult stem cells: Stem cells (cell with the potential to differentiate and form a variety of other cell types) that are found in small quantities in adult tissues.

Aerobic respiration: Breaking down food using oxygen to release energy for the cells.

Agar: The nutrient jelly on which many microorganisms are cultured.

Agglutinate: Stick together.

Agriculture: Growing plants or other organisms on farms to supply human needs e.g. for food, clothing etc.

Algal cells: The cells of algae, single-celled or simple multicellular organisms, which can photosynthesise but are not plants.

Allele: A version of a particular gene.

Alveoli: The tiny air sacs in the lungs that increase the surface area for gaseous exchange.

Amino acids: The building blocks of protein.

Amylase: The enzyme made in the salivary glands and the pancreas which speeds up the breakdown of starch into simple sugars.

Anaerobic respiration: Breaking down food without oxygen to release energy for the cells.

Anther: Makes pollen containing the male gametes of the plant.

Antibiotic: Drug that destroys bacteria inside the body without damaging human cells.

Antibodies: Proteins made by the white blood cells which bind to specific antigens.

Antigen: The unique protein on the surface of a cell. It is recognised by the immune system as 'self' or 'non-self'.

Aorta: The main artery leaving the left ventricle carrying oxygenated blood to the body.

Artery: Blood vessel which carries blood away from the heart. It has a pulse.

Artificial pacemaker: An electrical device that can be implanted to act as pacemaker for the heart when the natural pacemaker region fails.

Asexual budding: A form of asexual reproduction where a complete new individual forms as a bud on the parent organism e.g. yeast, hydra.

Asexual reproduction: Reproduction that involves only one individual with no fusing of gametes to produce the offspring. The offspring are identical to the parent.

Atrium: The small upper chambers of the heart. The right atrium receives blood from the body and the left atrium receives blood from the lungs.

Auxin: A plant hormone that controls the responses of plants to light (phototropism) and to gravity (gravitropism).

Bacteria: Single-celled microorganisms that can reproduce very rapidly. Many bacteria are useful, e.g. gut bacteria and decomposing bacteria, but some cause disease.

Bacterial colony: A population of billions of bacteria grown in culture.

Bases: Nitrogenous compounds that make up part of the structure of DNA and RNA.

Benign tumours: Tumours that grow in one location and do not invade other tissues.

Biconcave disc: The shape of the red blood cells – a disc that is dimpled inwards on both sides.

Bile: Yellowy-green liquid made in the liver and stored in the gall bladder. It is released into the small intestine, neutralises stomach acid and emulsifies fats.

Biodiversity: The number and variety of different organisms found in a specified area.

Biofuel: Fuel produced from biological material which is renewable and sustainable.

Biological detergent: Washing detergent that contains enzymes.

Biomass: Biological material from living or recently living organisms.

Biotic index of water cleanliness: A measure of how clean water is by studying the type and numbers of living organisms found in it.

Bladder: The organ where urine is stored until it is released from the body.

Blood: The liquid which is pumped around the body by the heart. It contains blood cells, dissolved food, oxygen, waste products, mineral ions, hormones and other substances needed in the body or needing to be removed from the body.

Blood circulation system: The system by which blood is pumped around the body.

Blood vessel: A tube which carries blood around the body, i.e. arteries, veins and capillaries.

Breathing: The physical movement of air into and out of the lungs. In humans this is brought about by the action of the intercostal muscles on the ribs and the diaphragm.

Callus: A mass of unspecialised plant tissue.

Cancer: The common name for a malignant tumour.

Capillaries: The smallest blood vessels which run between individual cells. They have a wall that is only one cell thick.

Carbohydrase: Enzyme that speeds up the breakdown of carbohydrates.

Carbohydrates: Molecules that provide us with energy. They contain the chemical elements carbon, hydrogen and oxygen and are made up of single sugar units.

Carbon cycle: The cycling of carbon through the living and non-living world.

Carbon sinks: Something that takes up more carbon dioxide than it produces e.g. plants, the oceans.

Carcinogens: Chemicals that can cause mutations in cells and so trigger the formation of malignant tumours.

Carnivore: Animal that eats other animals.

Carpel: The female parts of a flower made up of the stigma, style and ovary.

Carrier: Individual who is heterozygous for a faulty allele that causes a genetic disease in the homozygous form.

Catalyst: A substance which speeds up a chemical reaction. At the end of the reaction the catalyst remains chemically unchanged.

Cell cycle: The sequence of events by which cells grow and divide.

Cell membrane: The membrane around the contents of a cell that controls what moves in and out of the cell.

Cellulose: A big carbohydrate molecule that makes up plant and algal cell walls.

Cell wall: A rigid structure which surrounds the cells of living organisms apart from animals.

Central nervous system (CNS): The central nervous system is made up of the brain and spinal cord where information is processed.

Cerebellum: Region of the brain concerned with coordinating muscular activity and balance.

Cerebral cortex: Region of the brain concerned with consciousness, memory and language.

Charles Darwin: The Victorian scientist who developed the theory of evolution by a process of natural selection.

Chlorophyll: The green pigment contained in the chloroplasts.

Chloroplasts: The organelles in which photosynthesis takes place.

Chromosome: Thread-like structure carrying the genetic information found in the nucleus of a cell.

Classification: The organisation of living things into groups according to their similarities.

Clone: Offspring produced by asexual reproduction which is identical to its parent organism.

Cloning: The production of offspring that are genetically identical to the parent organism.

Combustion: The process of burning.

Competition: The process by which living organisms compete with each other for limited resources such as food, light or reproductive partners.

Complex carbohydrates: Carbohydrates made up of long chains of single sugar units e.g. starch, cellulose.

Compost heap: A site where garden rubbish and kitchen waste are decomposed by microorganisms.

Concentration gradient: The gradient between an area where a substance is at a high concentration and an area where it is at a low concentration.

Core body temperature: The internal temperature of the body.

Coronary artery: An artery which carries oxygenated blood to the muscle of the heart.

Coronary heart disease: Heart disease caused by problems with the coronary arteries that supply the heart muscle with oxygenated blood.

Culture medium: A substance containing the nutrients needed for microorganisms to grow.

Cuticle: The waxy covering of a leaf (or an insect) which reduces water loss from the surface.

Cystic fibrosis: A genetic disease that affects the lungs, digestive and reproductive systems. It is inherited through a recessive allele.

Cytoplasm: The water-based gel in which the organelles of all living cells are suspended.

Decomposer: Microorganism that breaks down waste products and dead bodies.

Deforestation: Removal of forests by felling, burning, etc.

Denatured: Change the shape of an enzyme so that it can no longer speed up a reaction.

Deoxygenated: Lacking in oxygen.

Detritivores: Organisms that feed on organic waste from animals and the dead bodies of animals and plants.

Detritus feeder: See detritivores.

Dialysis: The process of cleansing the blood through a dialysis machine when the kidneys have failed.

Dialysis machine: The machine used to remove urea and excess mineral ions from the blood when the kidneys fail.

Diaphragm: A strong sheet of muscle that separates the thorax from the digestive organs, used to change the volume of the chest during ventilation of the lungs.

Differentiate: Specialise for a particular function.

Diffusion: The net movement of particles of a gas or a solute from an area of high concentration to an area of low concentration (down a concentration gradient).

Digestive juices: The mixture of enzymes and other chemicals produced by the digestive system.

Digestive system: The organ system running from the mouth to the anus where food is digested.

Direct contact: A way of spreading infectious diseases by skin contact between two people.

DNA: Deoxyribonucleic acid, the material of inheritance.

Dominant: The characteristic that will show up in the offspring even if only one of the alleles is inherited.

Donor: The person who gives material from their body to another person who needs healthy tissues or organs, e.g. blood, kidneys. Donors may be alive or dead.

Double circulation: The separate circulation of the blood from the heart to the lungs and then back to the heart and on to the body.

Droplet infection: A way of spreading infectious diseases through the tiny droplets full of pathogens, which are expelled from your body when you cough, sneeze or talk.

Drug: A chemical which causes changes in the body. Medical drugs cure disease or relieve symptoms. Recreational drugs alter the state of your mind and/or body.

Ecology: The scientific study of the relationships between living organisms and their environment.

Effector organs: Muscles and glands which respond to impulses from the nervous system.

Egg nucleus: The nucleus of the female gamete that will form the embryo when it is fertilised.

Electron microscope: An instrument used to magnify specimens using a beam of electrons.

Element: A substance made up of only one type of atom. An element cannot be broken down chemically into any simpler substance.

Embryonic stem cell: Stem cell with the potential to form a number of different specialised cell types, which is taken from an early embryo.

Emulsify: Break down into tiny droplets which will form an emulsion.

Endemic: When a species evolves in isolation and is found in only one place in the world; it is said to be endemic (particular) to that area.

Endosperm nucleus: The nucleus of the female gamete that will form the endosperm (food store) when it is fertilised.

Environmental cause: External, not inherited condition that affects the way in which characteristics of organisms develop.

Enzyme: Protein molecule which acts as a biological catalyst. It changes the rate of chemical reactions without being affected itself at the end of the reaction.

Epidermal tissue: The tissue of the epidermis – the outer layer of an organism.

Epithelial tissue: Tissue made up of relatively unspecialised cells which line the tubes and organs of the body.

Eutrophication: The process by which excessive nutrients in water lead to very fast plant growth. When the plants die they are decomposed and this uses up a lot of oxygen so the water can no longer sustain animal life.

Evaporation: The change of a liquid to a vapour at a temperature below its boiling point.

Evolution: The process of slow change in living organisms over long periods of time as those best adapted to survive breed successfully.

Evolutionary relationship: Model of the relationships between organisms, often based on DNA evidence, which suggests how long ago they evolved away from each other and how closely related they are in evolutionary terms.

Evolutionary tree: Model of the evolutionary relationships between different organisms based on their appearance, and increasingly, on DNA evidence.

Exchange surface: A surface where materials are exchanged.

Extinction: Extinction is the permanent loss of all the members of a species.

Extremophile: Organism which lives in environments that are very extreme, e.g. very high or very low temperatures, high salt levels or high pressures.

False negative: A test that shows that a specific problem is not present when in fact it is.

False positive: A test that shows that a specific problem is present when it is not.

Fatty acids: Building blocks of lipids.

Fermentation: The reaction in which the enzymes in yeast turn glucose into ethanol and carbon dioxide.

Fertile: A fertile soil contains enough minerals e.g. nitrates, to supply the crop plants with the all nutrients needed for healthy growth.

Fertiliser: A substance provided for plants that supplies them with essential nutrients for healthy growth.

Filament: Attaches the anther to the flower.

Fossil: The remains of an organism from many thousands or millions of years ago that has been preserved in rock, ice, amber, peat, etc.

Fossil fuel: Fuel obtained from long-dead biological material.

Fructose syrup: A sugar syrup.

Gamete: Sex cell that has half the chromosome number of an ordinary cell.

Gametocyte: The stage in the lifecycle of the malaria parasite *Plasmodium* that reproduces sexually and infects female mosquitos.

Gaseous exchange: The exchange of gases, e.g. the exchange of oxygen and carbon dioxide which occurs between the air in the lungs and the blood.

Gene: A short section of DNA carrying genetic information to determine a characteristic.

Gene probe: A probe that will bind to a particular damaged gene or chromosome.

Genetically modified: An organism that has had its genetic material modified, usually by the addition of at least one new gene.

Genetically modified crops (GM crops): Crops that have had their genes modified by genetic engineering techniques.

Genetic cause: The allele inherited by an organism that determines its characteristics directly.

Genetic disorder: Disease that is inherited.

Genetic engineering: A technique for changing the genetic information of a cell.

Genetic material: The DNA which carries the instructions for making a new cell or a new individual.

Genotype: The genetic makeup of an individual regarding a particular characteristic.

Geographical isolation: This is when two populations become physically isolated by a geographical feature.

Glandular tissue: The tissue which makes up the glands and secretes chemicals, e.g. enzymes, hormones.

Global warming: Warming of the Earth due to greenhouse gases in the atmosphere trapping infrared radiation from the surface.

Glucose: A simple sugar.

Glycerol: Building block of lipids.

Glycogen: Carbohydrate store in animals, including the muscles, liver and brain of the human body.

Gravitropism: Response of a plant to the force of gravity controlled by auxin.

Greenhouse effect: The trapping of infrared radiation from the Sun as a result of greenhouse gases, such as carbon dioxide and methane, in the Earth's atmosphere. The greenhouse effect maintains the surface of the Earth at a temperature suitable for life.

Greenhouse gas: Gases, such as carbon dioxide and methane, which absorb infrared radiated from the Earth, and result in warming up the atmosphere.

Guard cells: The cells which surround stomata in the leaves of plants and control their opening and closing.

Haemoglobin: The red pigment which carries oxygen around the body.

Heart: The muscular organ which pumps blood around the body.

Herbicide: Chemical that kills plants.

Herbivore: Animal that feeds on plants.

Herd immunity: The target of vaccination programmes because when a large percentage of the population are immune to a disease, the spread of the pathogen is greatly reduced and it may disappear completely from a population.

Heterozygous: An individual with different alleles for a characteristic.

Homeostasis: The maintenance of constant internal body conditions.

Homozygous: An individual with two identical alleles for a characteristic.

Hormone: Chemical produced in glands that carries chemical messages around the body.

Horticulture: Growing plants for food and pleasure in gardens.

Hydrotropism: The response of a plant to water.

Hypertonic: A solution with a higher concentration of solute molecules than another solution.

Hypothermia: The state when the core body temperature falls below the normal range.

Hypotonic: A solution with a lower concentration of solute molecules than another solution.

Immune response: The response of the immune system to cells carrying foreign antigens. It results in the production of antibodies against the foreign cells and the destruction of those cells.

Immune system: The body system that recognises and destroys foreign cells or proteins such as invading pathogens.

Immunisation: Giving a vaccine that allows immunity to develop without exposure to the disease itself.

Immunosuppressant drug: Drug that suppresses the immune system of the recipient of a transplanted organ to prevent rejection.

Impulse: Electrical signal carried along the neurons.

Industrial waste: Waste produced by industrial processes.

Infectious: Capable of causing infection.

Infectious disease: Disease that can be passed from one individual to another.

Inheritance of acquired characteristics: Jean-Baptiste Lamarck's theory of how evolution took place.

Inherited disorder: Passed on from parents to their offspring through genes.

Inoculate: To make someone immune to a disease by injecting them with a vaccine which stimulates the immune system to make antibodies against the disease.

Insoluble molecule: Molecule which will not dissolve in a particular solvent such as water.

Intercostal muscle: A muscle between the ribs that raises and lowers them during breathing movements.

Internal environment: The conditions inside the body.

Ion: A charged particle produced by the loss or gain of electrons.

Ionising radiation: Radiation made of particles which produce ions in the materials that they pass through, which in turn can make them biologically active and may result in mutation and cancer.

Isomerase: An enzyme which converts one form of a molecule into another.

Isotonic: Having the same concentration of solutes as another solution.

Jean-Baptiste Lamarck: French biologist who developed a theory of evolution based on the inheritance of acquired characteristics.

Kidney: Organ which filters the blood and removes urea, excess salts and water.

Kidney transplant: Replacing failed kidneys with a healthy kidney from a donor

Kidney tubule: A structure in the kidney where substances are reabsorbed back into the blood.

Kingdom: The highest group in the classification system e.g. animals, plants.

Lactic acid: One product of anaerobic respiration. It builds up in muscles with exercise. Important in yoghurt and cheese making processes.

Light microscope: An instrument used to magnify specimens using lenses and light.

Limiting factor: Factor which limits the rate of a reaction, e.g. temperature, pH, light levels (photosynthesis).

Lipase: Enzyme which breaks down fats and oils into fatty acids and glycerol.

Lipid: Oil or fat.

Liver: A large organ in the abdomen which carries out a wide range of functions in the body.

Male nuclei: The nuclei found in pollen grains.

Malignant tumour: Tumour that can spread around the body, invading health tissues as well as splitting and forming secondary tumours.

Mean: The arithmetical average of a series of numbers.

Median: The middle value in a list of data.

Medulla: Region of the brain concerned with unconscious activities such as controlling the heart beat and breathing.

Meiosis: The two-stage process of cell division which reduces the chromosome number of the daughter cells. It is involved in making the gametes for sexual reproduction.

Merozoite: The stage in the lifecycle of the malaria parasite *Plasmodium* that is released from the liver to infect the red blood cells of the human host.

Metastase: The way that malignant tumours spread around the body.

Methane: A hydrocarbon gas with the chemical formula CH_4. It makes up the main flammable component of biogas.

Microorganism: Bacteria, viruses and other organisms that can only be seen using a microscope.

Mineral ion: Chemical needed in small amounts as part of a balanced diet to keep the body healthy.

Mitochondria: The site of aerobic cellular respiration in a cell.

Mitosis: Cell division where two genetically identical cells are formed.

Mode: The number which occurs most often in a set of data.

Molecule: A particle made up of two or more atoms bonded together.

Monitor: Observations made over a period of time.

Monohybrid crosses: Genetic crosses involving the inheritance of a single gene.

Motor neurone: Neurone that carries impulses from the central nervous system to the effector organs.

MRSA: Methicillin-resistant *Staphylococcus aureus*. An antibiotic-resistant bacterium.

Multicellular organism: An organism which is made up of many different cells which work together. Some of the cells are specialised for different functions in the organism.

Muscular tissue: The tissue which makes up the muscles. It can contract and relax.

Mutation: A change in the genetic material of an organism.

Mycoprotein: A food based on the fungus *Fusarium* that grows and reproduces rapidly. It means 'protein from fungus'.

Natural classification system: Classification system based on the similarities between different living organisms.

Natural selection: The process by which evolution takes place. Organisms produce more offspring than the environment can support so only those which are most suited to their environment – the 'fittest' – will survive to breed and pass on their useful characteristics.

Negative feedback system: A system of control based on an increase in one substance triggering the release of another substance which brings about a reduction in levels of the initial stimulus.

Negative pressure: A system when the external pressure is lower than the internal pressure.

Nerve: Bundles of hundreds or even thousands of neurones.

Nervous system: See Central nervous system.

Net movement: The overall movement of …

Neurone: Basic cell of the nervous system that carries minute electrical impulses around the body.

Nitrate ion: Ion that is needed by plants to make proteins.

Non-renewable: Something that cannot be replaced once it is used up.

Nucleus (of a cell): An organelle found in many living cells containing the genetic information.

Optic nerve: The nerve carrying impulses from the retina of the eye to the brain.

Organ: A group of different tissues working together to carry out a particular function.

Organ system: A group of organs working together to carry out a particular function.

Osmosis: The net movement of water from an area of high concentration (of water) to an area of low concentration (of water) down a concentration gradient.

Ova: Female sex cells (gametes) in animals.

Ovary: Female sex organ which contains the eggs and produces sex hormones during the menstrual cycle.

Ovule: The female gamete in a plant.

Oxygenated: Containing oxygen.

Oxygen debt: The extra oxygen that must be taken into the body after exercise has stopped to complete the aerobic respiration of lactic acid.

Oxyhaemoglobin: The molecule formed when haemoglobin binds to oxygen molecules.

Pacemaker: Something biological or artificial that sets the basic rhythm of the heart.

Palisade mesophyll: Upper layer of mesophyll tissue in plant leaves that contains many chloroplasts for photosynthesis.

Pancreas: A gland that produces the hormone insulin, glucagon and several digestive enzymes.

Parasite: Organism which lives in or on other living organisms and gets some or all of its nourishment from this host organism.

Partially permeable membrane: Allowing only certain substances to pass through.

Pathogen: Microorganism that causes disease.

Permanent vacuole: A space in the cytoplasm filled with cell sap which is there all the time.

Pesticide: Chemical that kills animals.

Petal: Feature of a plant adapted to contain the sex organs. May be brightly coloured or patterned to attract insects and other pollinators.

Phenotype: The physical appearance/ biochemistry of an individual regarding a particular characteristic.

Phloem tissue: The living transport tissue in plants which carries sugars around the plant.

Photosynthesis: The process by which plants make glucose using carbon dioxide, water and light energy.

Phototropism: The response of a plant to light, controlled by auxin.

Pigment: A coloured molecule.

Pituitary gland: Small gland in the brain which produces a range of hormones controlling body functions.

Plasma: The clear, yellow liquid part of the blood which carries dissolved substances and blood cells around the body.

Plasmid: Extra circle of DNA found in bacterial cytoplasm.

Plasmolysis: The state of a plant cell when large amounts of water have moved out by osmosis and the protoplasm shrinks and pulls away from the cell wall leaving visible gaps.

Platelet: Fragment of cell in the blood which is vital for the clotting mechanism to work.

Pollen tube: The tube that grows out of the pollen grain down the style and through which the male nuclei travel to the ovules.

Polydactyly: A genetic condition inherited through a dominant allele which results in extra fingers and toes.

Polytunnel: Large greenhouse made of plastic.

Positive pressure: A system where the external pressure is higher than the internal pressure.

Precise: A precise measurement is one in which there is very little spread about the mean value. Precision depends only on the extent of random errors – it gives no indication of how close results are to the true value.

Predator: An animal which preys on other animals for food.

Protease: An enzyme which breaks down proteins.

Protein synthesis: The process by which proteins are made on the ribosomes based on information from the genes in the nucleus.

Puberty: The stage of development when the sexual organs and the body become adult.

Pulmonary artery: The large blood vessel taking deoxygenated blood from the right ventricle of the heart to the lungs.

Pulmonary vein: The large blood vessel bringing blood into the left atrium of the heart from the lungs.

Pyramid of biomass: A model of the mass of biological material in the organisms at each level of a food chain.

Quadrat: A piece of apparatus for sampling organisms in the field.

Quantitative sampling: Sampling which records the numbers of organisms rather than just the type.

Range: The maximum and minimum values of the independent or dependent variables; important in ensuring that any pattern is detected.

Receptor: Special sensory cell that detects changes in the environment.

Recessive: The characteristic that will show up in the offspring only if both of the alleles are inherited.

Recipient: The person who receives a donor organ.

Red blood cell: Blood cell which contains the red pigment haemoglobin. It is biconcave discs in shape and gives the blood its red colour.

Reflex: Rapid automatic response of the nervous system that does not involve conscious thought.

Reflex arc: The sense organ, sensory neuron, relay neuron, motor neuron and effector organ which bring about a reflex action.

Repeatable: A measurement is repeatable if the original experimenter repeats the investigation using same method and equipment and obtains the same results.

Reproducible: A measurement is reproducible if the investigation is repeated by another person, or by using different equipment or techniques, and the same results are obtained.

Respiration: The process by which food molecules are broken down to release energy for the cells.

Respiratory (breathing) system: The system of the body including the airways and lungs that is specially adapted for the exchange of gases between the air and the blood.

Ribosome: The site of protein synthesis in a cell.

Root hair cell: Cell on the root of a plant with microscopic hairs which increases the surface area for the absorption of water from the soil.

Salivary gland: Gland in the mouth which produces saliva containing the enzyme amylase.

Sample size: The size of a sample in an investigation.

Schizont: The stage in the lifecycle of the malaria parasite *Plasmodium* that bursts out of the red blood cells, destroying them and causing symptoms of disease.

Selective reabsorption: The process by which all the glucose and varying amounts of water and mineral ions are absorbed back into the blood from the kidney tubule.

Sense organ: Organ containing a collection of special cells known as receptors which responds to changes in the surroundings (e.g. eye, ear).

Sensory neurones: Neurone which carries impulses from the sensory organs to the central nervous system.

Sepal: Small green leaf-like structures that protect a flower when it is in bud.

Sequestered: The storage of carbon dioxide directly or indirectly in plant material and water.

Sewage: A combination of bodily waste, waste water from homes and rainfall overflow from street drains.

Sewage treatment plant: A site where human waste is broken down using microorganisms.

Sex chromosome: A chromosome which carries the information about the sex of an individual.

Sexual reproduction: Reproduction which involves the joining (fusion) of male and female gametes producing genetic variety in the offspring.

Sickle-cell anaemia: A genetic disorder affecting the structure of the haemoglobin which in turn affects the shape of the red blood cells, making them sickle shaped so they don't carry oxygen efficiently.

Simple sugars: Small carbohydrate molecules made up of single sugar units or two sugar units joined together.

Sinoatrial node: The region of the special tissue that acts as the natural pacemaker region of the heart.

Small intestine: The region of the digestive system where most of the digestion of the food takes place.

Smog: A haze of small particles and acidic gases that form in the air over major cities as a result of the burning of fossil fuels in vehicles and pollution from industrial processes.

Solar (light) energy: Energy from the Sun.

Solute: The solid which dissolves in a solvent to form a solution.

Specialised: Adapted for a particular function.

Speciation: The formation of a new species.

Species: A group of organisms with many features in common which can breed successfully producing fertile offspring.

Sperm: Male sex cell (gamete) in animals.

Spongy mesophyll: Lower layer of mesophyll tissue in plant leaves that contains some chloroplasts and also has big air spaces to give a large surface area for the diffusion of gases.

Sporozoite: The stage in the lifecycle of the malaria parasite *Plasmodium* that is passed on to humans when the female mosquito takes a blood meal. This goes on to infect the liver.

Stamen: The male part of a flower made up of the anthers and filament.

Stem cell: Undifferentiated cell with the potential to form a wide variety of different cell types.

Stent: A metal mesh placed in the artery which is used to open up the blood vessel by the inflation of a tiny balloon.

Stigma: The part of the flower where pollen lands during pollination.

Stimuli: A change in the environment that is detected by sensory receptors.

Stomata: Openings in the leaves of plants (particularly the underside) which allow gases to enter and leave the leaf. They are opened and closed by the guard cells.

Style: The part that transports the male sex cells to the ovary.

Sulfur dioxide: A polluting gas formed when fossil fuels containing sulfur impurities are burned.

Sustainable food production: Methods of producing food which can be sustained over time without destroying the fertility of the land or ocean.

Synapse: A gap between neurones where the transmission of information is chemical rather than electrical.

Territory: An area where an animal lives and feeds, which it may mark out or defend against other animals.

Therapeutic cloning: Cloning by transferring the nucleus of an adult cell to an empty egg to produce tissues or organs which could be used in medicine.

Thermoregulatory centre: The area of the brain which is sensitive to the temperature of the blood.

Thorax: The upper (chest) region of the body. In humans it includes the ribcage, heart and lungs.

Tissue: A group of specialised cells all carrying out the same function.

Tissue culture: Using small groups of cells from a plant to make new plants.

Trachea: The main tube lined with cartilage rings which carries air from the nose and mouth down towards the lungs.

Transect: A measured line or area along which ecological measurements (e.g. quadrats) are made.

Translocation: The movement of sugars from the leaves to the rest of a plant.

Transpiration: The loss of water vapour from the leaves of plants through the stomata when they are opened to allow gas exchange for photosynthesis.

Transpiration stream: The movement of water through a plant from the roots to the leaves as a result of the loss of water by evaporation from the surface of the leaves.

Transport system: A system for transporting substances around a multicellular living organism.

Tropism: The response of a plant to a stimulus by growth e.g. phototropism.

Tuber: Modified part of a plant which is used to store food in the form of starch.

Tumour: A mass of abnormally growing cells that form when the cells do not respond to the normal mechanisms which control the cell cycle.

Urea: The waste product formed by the breakdown of excess amino acids in the liver.

Urine: The liquid produced by the kidneys containing the metabolic waste product urea along with excess water and salts from the body.

Vaccination: Introducing small quantities of dead or inactive pathogens into the body to stimulate the white blood cells to produce antibodies that destroy the pathogens. This makes the person immune to future infection.

Vaccine: The dead or inactive pathogen material used in vaccination.

Vacuum: An area with little or no gas pressure.

Valid: Suitability of the investigative procedure to answer the question being asked.

Valve: Structure which prevents the backflow of liquid, e.g. the valves of the heart or the veins.

Variable: Physical, chemical or biological quantity or characteristic.

Vein: Blood vessel which carries blood away from the heart. It has valves to prevent the backflow of blood.

Vena cava: The large vein going into the right atrium of the heart carrying deoxygenated blood from the body.

Ventilated: Movement of air into and out of the lungs.

Ventricle: A large chamber at the bottom of the heart. The right ventricle pumps blood to the lungs, the left ventricle pumps blood around the body.

Villi: The finger-like projections from the lining of the small intestine which increase the surface area for the absorption of digested food into the blood.

Virus: Microorganism which takes over body cells and reproduces rapidly, causing disease.

White blood cell: Blood cells involved in the immune system of the body. Some engulf pathogens, others produce antibodies or antitoxins.

Wilting: The process by which plants droop when they are short of water or too hot. This reduces further water loss and prevents cell damage.

Xylem tissue: The non-living transport tissue in plants, which transports water and mineral ions around the plant.

Yeast: Single-celled fungi which produce ethanol when they respire carbohydrates anaerobically.

Zygote: Cell formed when the male and female gametes fuse.

Answers

1 Cell activity

▶ 1.1
1 Mitochondria
2 Absorb light for photosynthesis.
3 Onion cells do not have chloroplasts for photosynthesis because they are underground and do not receive light.

▶ 1.2
1 In the cytoplasm (a bacterium does not have a nucleus).
2 Anaerobic respiration

▶ 1.3
1 Muscle cells need a lot of energy for movement. Energy release occurs in mitochondria.
2 Increases the surface area of the root hair cell.
3 A cell that shows all the usual features of a cell but does not have specialised features (usually a diagram).

▶ 1.4
1 The concentration of the particles on either side of the membrane.
2 Carbon dioxide

▶ 1.5
1 Partially permeable
2 Isotonic
3 a The sugar solution inside the bag is more concentrated than the water outside the bag. Water moves into the bag by osmosis.
   b The solution outside the bag is more concentrated than the water inside the bag, so water moves out of the bag by osmosis.

▶ 1.6
1 The particles are being absorbed **against** a concentration gradient.
2 Mineral ions

▶ 1.7
1 Large organisms have a small surface area to volume ratio. Exchange surfaces allow materials to be passed to a transport system which carries materials to all the cells.
2 The leaves are flat and thin, have internal air spaces and stomata.

▶ 1.8
1 Any two of: large surface area, thin walls, good blood supply.
2 One of: sugar/glucose, amino acids, fatty acids, glycerol, vitamins, minerals, water.

Answers to end of Chapter 1 questions

1 a Chloroplasts, cell wall, permanent vacuole
  b Chloroplasts
2 To produce protein
3 Diffusion is the movement of all types of particle from a region of high to low concentration. Osmosis is the movement of water from a dilute solution to a concentrated solution across a partially permeable membrane.
4 A solution with a lower concentration of solute molecules than another solution.
5 Villi
6 Large surface area, thin walls or short diffusion path, good transport system.
7 Active transport requires energy; movement of particles is against the diffusion gradient – diffusion does not require energy and particles move down the concentration gradient.
8 a Absorption of mineral ions by roots
  b Absorption of glucose out of the gut or from kidney tubules into the blood
9 The roots are long and thin and there are thousands of root hair cells on the ends of the roots. Increases the surface area for absorption of water and mineral ions.
10 Sea water contains salt so the solution around the animal is hypertonic (more concentrated). Water leaves the cells by osmosis so chemical reactions in cytoplasm stop.
11 Water moves out of the cell from a more dilute solution to the more concentrated solution. The vacuole and cytoplasm shrink, so the cell membrane draws away from the wall and the cell becomes plasmolysed.

2 Cell division, differentiation and organisation

▶ 2.1
1 Mitosis
2 They appear as thin threads.

▶ 2.2
1 Gametes or sex cells, the eggs and sperm
2 There are two sets of cell division. A body cell divides into two and each divides again.

▶ 2.3
1 Change into a specialised cell from a stem cell.
2 Bone marrow (there may be stem cells in other tissues, e.g. liver)

▶ 2.4
1 A mass of abnormally growing cells which are dividing in an uncontrolled way.
2 Carcinogens and ionising radiation

▶ 2.5
1 Enzymes or hormones
2 Photosynthesis

▶ 2.6
1 Biological catalysts
2 The small intestine

Answers to end of Chapter 2 questions

1 Any three of: salivary glands, pancreas, stomach, liver, small intestine, large intestine.
2 Epidermal tissue, palisade mesophyll, spongy mesophyll, xylem, phloem
3 Different forms (versions) of a particular gene.
4 Mitosis
5 Embryos and bone marrow
6 Cells become specialised for a particular function.
7 A tumour which can spread around the body and invade healthy tissue.
8 Meiosis
9 They are produced by mitosis. Cells from one parent divide to produce identical cells.
10 When meiosis occurs to form the gametes, each gamete is genetically different. Then the female gamete (egg) fuses with a male gamete (sperm). The zygote contains chromosomes with genes from both parents.
11 The insoluble food is mixed with digestive juices produced by glands. It is digested by enzymes in the stomach and small intestine. Bile produced by the liver is added to the food to help lipid digestion. Absorption of the soluble food takes place in the small intestine. Water is absorbed by the large intestine.

3 Carbohydrates, lipids, proteins and enzymes

▶ 3.1
1 A long chain of simple sugar units bonded/linked together.
2 It changes shape and is denatured.
3 a Iodine solution stays brown/orange.
   b Benedict's solution would remain clear blue.
   c Biuret solution would turn lilac.

▶ 3.2
1 The active site
2 Catalase works faster than manganese(IV) oxide. The graph shows a steeper curve for liver + hydrogen peroxide which reaches the end point before the manganese(IV) oxide.

▶ 3.3
1 Changing the shape of the active site so the enzyme can no longer speed up a reaction
2 Breakdown of large insoluble molecules to smaller soluble molecules

▶ 3.4
1 Isomerase
2 The egg will get smaller because it will be digested.

3 **a** Weigh the egg white before and after the investigation.
   b Use the same weight but different shapes of egg white – e.g. thin and flat versus cubes.
   c Proteases could digest skin cells or irritate the skin.

Answers to end of Chapter 3 questions

1 pH and temperature
2 Fatty acid and glycerol
3 Amino acids
4 Any three of: structural components of tissues, e.g. muscles and tendons; act as hormones; form antibodies; act as biological catalysts – enzymes are made of protein.
5 The optimum temperature
6 The protease is used to pre-digest proteins so the baby can absorb them more easily.
7 Any two of: builds large molecules from smaller molecules, changes one molecule into another, breaks down large molecules into smaller molecules.
8 The molecules have more energy; therefore, they move around faster and collide more often so there are more collisions in a given time.
9 The enzyme and the substrate molecules will move faster so the substrate will collide with the active site more often up to a certain temperature. However, higher temperatures change the shape of the enzyme's active site and it becomes denatured.
10 Advantage: less energy or less expensive equipment is needed because the reactions can take place at normal temperature and pressure.
    Disadvantage: costly to produce, denatured at high temperatures.
11 The enzymes speed up the digestion of stains from food, blood and grass, and therefore lower temperatures can be used in washing machines.

Answers to examination-style questions

1 **a** X = cell membrane   (1)
   b **i**   propels the sperm/for swimming   (1)
          ii they release energy/they respire   (1)
                  the energy is needed to move the tail   (1)
          iii the sperm must penetrate an egg   (1)
                  the enzymes digest the outer layers of the egg   (1)
          iv meiosis   (1)
   c **i**   Root hair cell has nucleus, cell membrane, cytoplasm
                  (all three answer = *2 marks*, two answers = *1 mark*)
          ii has a cell wall and vacuole   (2)
2 **a** selectively permeable, diffusion, high, cytoplasm, osmosis, low   (6)
   b mucus blocks surface of intestine/stomach/pancreatic duct   (1)
          digestive enzymes cannot reach the food   (1)
   c very little soluble food materials can be absorbed (1), cells cannot develop/idea of no growth (1), oxygen cannot diffuse into bloodstream (1), little respiration (1), increased risk of lung infection (1)
3 **a** Water would diffuse out into the salt (1) due to the difference in concentration/osmosis (1), so cytoplasm would be dehydrated and/or unsuitable for chemical reactions   (1)
   b Swell/burst   (1)
   c (Would expect) enzymes to denature so no chemical reactions could occur   (2)
4 Any four of: cells multiply (1) and push through the layers of skin/break through the skin (1), the cancer cells enter the bloodstream and are carried to the liver (1), the cells attach to the liver and multiply (1) forming a new tumour (in the liver)   (1)

4 Human biology – breathing

4.1
1 Intercostal muscles and diaphragm
2 Alveoli

4.2
1 One of: if the alveoli are damaged, if the tubes leading to the lungs are narrowed, if the person is paralysed.
2 Iron lung

4.3
1 Mitochondria
2 Protein is a large molecule made by combining many smaller molecules.
3 Without oxygen the organism would die.

4.4
1 Glucose
2 The fit person has more blood pumped per heart beat, a bigger heart volume at rest, a lower breathing rate, a lower pulse rate.

4.5
1 Lactic acid
2 They start to feel fatigued/muscles ache.

Answers to end of Chapter 4 questions

1 Carbon dioxide and water.
2 Respiration without using oxygen.
3 Glucose and oxygen.
4 Large surface area, thin walls in close contact with blood capillaries (short diffusion path), well supplied with blood capillaries (for transport/to maintain a steep diffusion gradient).
5 Any three of: build larger molecules from smaller ones; enable muscle contraction in animals; maintain a constant body temperature in mammals and birds; active transport; build sugars, nitrates and other nutrients into amino acids and then proteins in plants.
6 $C_6H_{12}O_6 \rightarrow 2C_2H_5OH + 2CO_2$
7 Lactic acid builds up in the muscles.
8 The breathing rate and heart rate increase.
9 This allows an increased blood supply to the muscle cells to provide oxygen and glucose more quickly and to remove carbon dioxide faster.
10 The amount of oxygen needed to break down the lactic acid produced in anaerobic respiration.
11 The intercostal muscles contract, the diaphragm contracts. The ribcage moves up and out, the diaphragm flattens. This increases the volume inside the thorax and decreases the pressure, so air is forced into the lungs.
12 Any one of: it is much smaller/the person does not have to lie in a metal case/some can be used in the home/they can be controlled by computers to give the correct amount of air.

5 Human biology – circulation and digestion

5.1
1 They prevent blood from flowing in the wrong direction.
2 The heart is two pumps attached together, one pump (right) pumps blood to the lungs, the other pump (left) pumps blood to the rest of the body.

5.2
1 Right atrium

5.3
1 Arteries have thicker walls than veins. Veins have valves along their length, arteries do not have valves along their length.
2 To open up blood vessels which have been narrowed by fatty deposits, particularly the coronary arteries.
3 The heart rate/heart beats

5.4
1 Carbon dioxide
2 They help the blood to clot at the site of a wound.

5.5
1 Blood group O
2 Immunosuppressant drugs

5.6
1 The villi have a large surface area, are well supplied with blood capillaries, have thin walls.
2 Protease
3 **a** Iodine solution turns blue/black.
   b Benedict's reagent turns from clear blue to a red/orange precipitate when boiled with sample.

5.7
1 To increase the surface area of the fat droplets so lipase can digest them quicker
2 The hydrochloric acid alone has not digested the meat. The pepsin has started the digestion of the meat but at a slow rate. The pepsin with the acid (low pH) has worked efficiently and digested the meat because the pH is optimum for the pepsin to work.

Answers to end of Chapter 5 questions

1 Amylase
2 a Liver
 b Gall bladder
3 Valves
4 Small intestine (and stomach)
5 The molecules are too big to pass across the cell membranes in the gut wall.
6 a Amino acids
 b Fatty acids and glycerol
7 Neutralises the stomach acid, makes the conditions in the small intestine slightly alkaline, emulsifies fats to increase the surface area of the fats for lipase enzymes to act upon.
8 Controls the resting heart rate
9 A metal mesh which is inserted into a narrowed artery to open it up, allowing the blood to flow freely through the artery.
10 Vena cava → right atrium → right ventricle → pulmonary artery → lungs → pulmonary vein → left atrium → left ventricle → aorta
11 Blood group O can be given to people with any of the ABO groups. Because there are no antigens on the red blood cells they will not cause the blood cells to stick together (to agglutinate).
12 They suppress the immune system, therefore the person may not produce antibodies to combat infectious diseases.

6 Nervous coordination

⫸ 6.1
1 Light, sound, chemicals, touch, pain and temperature changes
2 Electrical impulse

⫸ 6.2
1 Along a sensory neurone
2 It acts as a coordinator, linking the sensory and motor neurones.

⫸ 6.3
1 Cerebellum
2 MRI (magnetic resonance imaging)

Answers to end of Chapter 6 questions

1 Any three of: light, sound, chemicals, touch, pain, pressure, changes in position, temperature changes.
2 Muscles – contract; glands – secrete hormones
3 A chemical is secreted from a neurone which diffuses/spreads to another neurone.
4 An automatic, rapid response to a stimulus
5 Cerebral cortex
6 They help you to avoid /protect you from danger.
7 Any two of: heartbeat, breathing, movements of the gut.
8 Any two of: studying patients with brain damage, electrically stimulating different parts of the brain, using MRI scanning techniques.
9 a Receptors in the ear
 b Receptors in nose and on tongue
 c Receptors in skin
10 Stimulus → receptor → sensory neurone → coordinator (relay neurone) → motor neurone → effector → response
11 The brain must receive stimuli from all body activities so that it can coordinate all movements/activities.
12 The pain receptors in that region of the skin have been damaged.

Answers to examination-style questions

1 a Pulling hand away from a very hot plate. Blinking when a bright light is shone in the eyes. Coughing when a crumb enters the trachea. (3)
 b Breathing, moving food through your gut (1)
 c You do them automatically/you do not have to think about them/they are fast (1)
 d Cerebral cortex (1)
2 a A. No mark – can be specified in reason part. [If B given, no marks throughout; if unspecified plus two good reasons, 1 mark.]
 High(er) pressure in A (1) [Allow opposite for B, do not accept 'zero pressure' for B]
 Pulse/described in A (1) [Accept fluctuates/'changes', allow reference to beats/beating, ignore reference to artery pumping]

b i 17 (1)
 ii 68 (1)
 [Accept correct answer from student's (b)(i) × 4]
c i Oxygen/oxygenated blood (1)
 [Allow adrenaline, ignore air]
 glucose/sugar (1)
 [Extra wrong answer cancels, e.g. sucrose/starch/glycogen/glucagon/water, allow fructose as an alternative to glucose, ignore energy, ignore food]
 ii Carbon dioxide/CO_2/lactic acid (1)
 [Allow CO2/CO^2, ignore water]
3 a i The thermometers have to be lifted out of the peas to read them (1), so the temperature reading will go down (1)
 ii Use a temperature probe (1) attached to a data logger (1)
 b i The thermometers stick out of the flask/can be read without moving them (1) they can be read without removing them from the peas (1)
 ii Air/oxygen cannot diffuse into the flask/carbon dioxide cannot diffuse out of the flask (1)
 c i Microorganisms (1) will decay the peas (1), respiration (of the microorganisms) releases more energy than respiration by the peas (1)
 ii Soak the peas in a disinfectant/named disinfectant (1) to kill the microorganisms (1)

7 Homeostasis

⫸ 7.1
1 So that the enzymes will work properly, too low they stop working, too high they denature
2 Pancreas

⫸ 7.2
1 In the cells during respiration
2 In the liver

⫸ 7.3
1 Filtration and (selective) reabsorption
2 A hormone (that controls the concentration of water in the blood) produced by the pituitary gland.

⫸ 7.4
1 Dialysis removes urea from the blood and restores normal concentrations of substances in the blood.
2 Kidney transplant

⫸ 7.5
1 Proteins on the surface of cells
2 The patient does not have to be attached to a machine every few days.

⫸ 7.6
1 The thermoregulatory centre in the brain
2 The water in the sweat evaporates. Energy from the skin is used to turn the water into water vapour so the skin cools.

⫸ 7.7
1 Insulin
2 Glucagon

⫸ 7.8
1 Any two of: pancreas transplants; transplanting pancreas cells; using embryonic stem cells to produce insulin secreting cells; using adult stem cells from diabetic patients; genetically engineering pancreas cells to make them work properly.
2 One of: help insulin to work better, help pancreas to produce insulin, reduce amount of sugar absorbed by the gut.

Answers to end of Chapter 7 questions

1 Excess amino acids are deaminated and the ammonia that is made is converted to urea (in the liver).
2 Respiration
3 Maintaining a constant internal environment
4 Any two of: makes urea, detoxifies poisons such as ethanol, breaks down red blood cells and stores iron.
5 In the brain
6 There are receptors in the pancreas to detect glucose levels.
7 Active transport
8 Glucagon is a hormone, produced by the pancreas which causes blood sugar to rise by converting glycogen to glucose. Glycogen is a storage carbohydrate found in the liver and muscles.

9 The blood has a lower solute concentration (more water) and receptors in the brain detect this. Less ADH is released, so less water is reabsorbed by the kidneys, so more water is lost in the urine – the urine is more dilute.

10 Eat a balanced diet/control carbohydrate intake, and do regular exercise to prevent becoming overweight.

11 If the machine contained water, most of the solutes would diffuse out of the plasma, e.g. glucose and mineral ions as well as urea. Water would enter the blood by osmosis and also enter the cells, damaging them.

8 Defending ourselves against disease

8.1
1 Pathogens produce toxins/damage cells.
2 No one knew about bacteria and viruses.

8.2
1 The skin stops pathogens entering, also mucus, stomach acid.
2 They ingest pathogens, produce antibodies, produce antitoxins.

8.3
1 Injection/oral drops of a dead or inactive pathogen to stimulate the white blood cells to produce antibodies.
2 By their shape

8.4
1 Viruses are inside body cells.

8.5
1 Very few people are immune to the new pathogen and no effective treatment is available.
2 Antibiotics kill the non-resistant strains which allows the resistant strains to survive and multiply (no competition).

8.6
1 The bacteria will grow at a faster rate.
2 Heat/sterilise all equipment, boil solutions, cover Petri dishes or flasks.
3 There is a clear area around the filter paper disc.

Answers to end of Chapter 8 questions

1 A microorganism which causes disease.
2 Any four from: use a handkerchief when coughing or sneezing, prevent direct/sexual contact with infected person, treat drinking water, cook food thoroughly, wash hands thoroughly, protect cuts to skin, treat surfaces/skin with antiseptics/disinfectants, prevent contact between raw and cooked food, avoid warm stuffy or crowded places during epidemics, any sensible reason.
3 Viruses reproduce inside cells. Medicines would damage the cells as well as the virus.
4 Genetic material/DNA
5 If they cause disease and there is no antibiotic/vaccine to treat them
6 Antibiotics kill pathogens inside the body. Antiseptics are used to kill pathogens in the environment.
7 A solution/agar jelly containing a population of only one species/type of bacterium
8 a To kill microorganisms
  b Otherwise it would kill bacteria in culture
  c To prevent microorganisms from the air entering
  d To reduce the risk of growing pathogens (human pathogens grow well at body temperature/37 °C)
9 Some bacteria mutate. The mutation may be resistant. Antibiotics kill the non-resistant strain. The resistant strain multiplies and survives. The number of resistant bacteria increases every time the antibiotic is used. Eventually the whole population is resistant.
10 Dead or inactive pathogen, which has the same shape molecule as antigen of the pathogen.
11 The vaccine enters the blood. White blood cells produce antibodies to destroy the specific pathogen. If the person is infected with this pathogen at a future date, the white blood cells respond quickly to produce more antibodies to destroy the live pathogen.

9 Plants as organisms

9.1
1 Sunlight
2 Brown/orange. No starch present as no photosynthesis in the dark.
3 The bubbles of gas can be seen and collected.

9.2
1 The activity of enzymes which control photosynthesis slows down at lower temperatures.
2 Oxygen

9.3
1 Starch, fats and oils
2 A plant which captures animals, e.g. insects and digests them.

9.4
1 To allow gases to diffuse in and out of the leaf
2 The stomata close to stop diffusion of water out of the leaf.

9.5
1 Diffusion
2 Any one of: more wind, increased temperature, drier.

9.6
1 Xylem and phloem
2 Change the conditions, e.g. use a hot/cold hairdryer, see how far the dye moves up the celery in a given time

9.7
1 Unequal distribution of auxin causes unequal growth of the shoot.
2 Towards the hole

9.8
1 The hormones might kill trees or other plants as well as weeds.
2 The broad-leaved plants have a bigger surface area and absorb more weed killer, so they go into uncontrolled growth and die.

9.9
1 Anther
2 To attract insects so they pick up pollen when they feed on the nectar.

9.10
1 Two
2 The ovary

Answers to end of Chapter 9 questions

1 Temperature, light intensity and time of lighting, carbon dioxide
2 Add iodine solution; the solution turns blue-black if starch is present.
3 a Water and mineral ions
  b Dissolved sugars
4 $6CO_2 + 6H_2O \xrightarrow{\text{light energy}} C_6H_{12}O_6 + 6O_2$
5 It will be hot enough anyway, so it would be a waste of energy. Photosynthesis may stop if the temperature becomes too high.
6 Factors, such as light, temperature and carbon dioxide, which might prevent the rate of photosynthesis increasing above a certain point
7 It catches insects, digests them and uses the mineral ions such as nitrates to make protein.
8 If the cells lose a lot of water, they become flaccid. To reduce water loss the stomata close. The leaves 'collapse', which reduces surface area so less water evaporates and diffuses out of the leaf.
9 As a rooting powder or a weed killer
10 The auxin accumulates on the lower side of the root, the cells on the upper side grow more (where there is least auxin) so the root bends downwards.
11 A pollen tube grows through the carpel's style into the ovule.
   The male nuclei from the pollen grain migrate into the ovule to fertilise the egg nucleus and endosperm nuclei.
   The resulting zygote develops into an embryo and the endosperm forms a food store.
   The endosperm and the female tissues of the ovule give rise to a seed.
   The ovary then grows into a fruit, which surrounds the seed(s).
12 Pollination is the transfer of pollen from the anther to the stigma. Fertilisation occurs when the male nuclei fuse with the female nuclei.

Answers to examination-style questions

1 a Some diseases are caused by bacteria (1) antibiotics kill bacteria (1)
  b Viruses reproduce inside cells (1) so the drugs/medicine would have to damage the cells to reach the viruses (1)
  c

0 marks	Level 1 (1–2 marks)	Level 2 (3–4 marks)	Level 3 (5–6 marks)
No relevant content	There is a description of at least one curve	There is a clear description of the two curves	There is a clear and detailed scientific description of the two curves and a reference to the fact that the fungus must grow before it can produce penicillin

Examples of student answers:
Fungus is growing during day 1.
After day 2 the growth has reached an optimum.
Penicillin production starts at (end) of day 1.
The rate increases (rapidly).
Rate doubles between day 2 and day 3.
After day 3 the rate of production slows down.
Reaches a maximum by day 5.
Idea that the nutrients are used in fungus growth before penicillin production.

2 a The label line must touch an anther (1)
  b Ovule (1)
  c Ovary (1)
  d i   By insects
     ii Large/colourful petals
     iii Any one of: nectar, scent (3)
  e endosperm, fertilisation, zygote, embryo, fruit (5)
3 a glucose passes into the villi (1)
  b pancreas (1)
  c glucagon (1)

10 Variation and inheritance

10.1
1 In the chromosomes
2 Genes control the development of characteristics (such as eye colour or thumb shape).

10.2
1 Asexual reproduction, because there is only one parent
2 Sexual reproduction, because the offspring has genes from both the mother and the father

10.3
1 The genes we inherit and environmental causes, e.g. diet
2 Availability of light, nutrients and space

10.4
1 X and Y
2 Genes

10.5
1 Three bases
2 Family tree or Punnett square

10.6
1 Polydactyly, other correct ones include Huntington's disease
2 50%, 2/4

10.7
1 Red blood cells (become sickle-shaped)

10.8
1 A chemical probe which will bind to a specific gene
2 Tests are carried out on the embryo to diagnose possible disorders.

Answers to end of Chapter 10 questions

1 The physical appearance of the characteristic
2 An extra chromosome 21, resulting in 47 chromosomes
3 Zygote
4 DNA
5 Alternative forms of a gene
6 The genetic material from two parents is brought together when the sperm and egg nuclei fuse.

7 They are produced by mitosis. Cells from only one parent divide to produce identical cells.
8 They have two different alleles of the same gene for a particular characteristic.
9 50%, as the dominant gene controls the condition; a child has a 50 : 50 chance of inheriting the allele from the heterozygous parent.
10 If both parents are heterozygous and pass the recessive allele to their child who is therefore homozygous recessive.
11 The gene contains the genetic code. The DNA in the gene is made of a sequence of bases. Three bases form the code for a particular amino acid. The sequence of groups of three bases determines the sequence of amino acids in the protein.

11 Genetic manipulation

11.1
1 Take cuttings from mature plants
2 Animal embryos must be split into groups of cells and then each group is transplanted into a host 'mother'. There have to be enough hosts and some embryos may die during development. It also takes longer for the animals to develop.

11.2
1 An adult cell such as a skin cell, and an egg cell
2 Any one of: save animals from extinction, production of proteins for use in medicine.

11.3
1 Enzymes
2 They may not be killed by herbicides, or they may be modified to kill pests that eat them.

11.4
1 GM crops should give a higher yield and therefore more money for the farmer.

Answers to end of Chapter 11 questions

1 Individuals who are genetically identical (to their parents)
2 Identical twins are genetically identical to each other, because they develop from the same fertilised egg when the embryo splits into two. (They are not identical to either parent though.)
3 Take cuttings
4 Tissue culture
5 A gene in an organism has been changed
6 The method by which genes are transferred from one organism to another to change the genetic make-up of the second organism.
7 Any three of: insulin can be produced in large quantities, antibodies can be produced to treat disease, genetic disorders can be treated, herbicide-resistant crops can be produced, insect-resistant crops can be produced, food that lasts longer can be produced. Other examples are possible but check they are correct.
8 After sexual reproduction, a single embryo is produced. The early embryo is split into several groups of cells. Each group is transplanted into a different host mother.
9 Cattle only have one or two young per year. If two prize animals are bred together, the farmer can get large numbers of prize calves by cloning the single embryo. Embryos can be flown around the world to benefit other farmers. Embryo cloning is a quicker, cheaper way to obtain large numbers of top-class cattle.
10 The gene is cut from the chromosome of the fish using enzymes. The fish gene is inserted into a vector (plasmid or virus), also using enzymes. The vector is used to transfer the fish gene into a chromosome of the tomato.

12 Adaptation and interdependence

12.1
1 A feature which allows the organism to live in its normal environment.
2 Organisms that live in extreme environmental conditions such as extreme cold, extreme heat, very salty or high pressure.

12.2
1 They have a small surface area to volume ratio.
2 To stay cool and to conserve water

12.3
1 They may have curled leaves, stomata situated away from heat and wind, waxy leaves, small leaves, water storage in the stems.

2 Plants may have thorns, poisonous chemicals or warning colours to stop animals eating them.

▶ 12.4

1 So they can find enough food and water. They also need space or shelter to protect and rear their young. Marking territory keeps out competitors.
2 The predator is put off by the warning colour of the caterpillar, which may be the same as a poisonous one.

▶ 12.5

1 To reduce competition for water, light, space and mineral ions.
2 Space if they are overcrowded, also light, nutrients and water.

▶ 12.6

1 Hooks and suckers on the head
2 Gametocytes, sporozoites, merozoites, schizonts

Answers to end of Chapter 12 questions

1 Adaptations allow organisms to survive in a particular habitat.
2 The process by which living organisms compete with each other for limited resources.
3 Water, food, space, mates and breeding sites. Their territory must be large enough to supply these.
4 To get enough light for photosynthesis, water and nutrients before the trees are active and the leaves shadow the small plants
5 Animals are coloured to blend in with their environment – camouflage means predators and prey are not easily seen by each other.
6 Any one from: extensive root system; roots go deep into soil; roots spread out; roots have root hair cells.
7 Has sharp, sucking mouthparts; flattened body; hard body; long legs
8 The tapeworm is surrounded by soluble food material in the host's intestine. It has a large surface area to absorb this food.
9 To continue the life cycle the eggs have to be eaten by another host animal which must come into contact with infected faeces.
10 Gametocytes – human blood and mosquito saliva; sporozoites – human blood and liver; merozoites – liver, red blood cells, blood; schizonts – red blood cells and released into blood

Answers to examination-style questions

1 a Liver and muscles (1)
  b Carbohydrase/enzyme (1)
  c Parent genotypes Gg and Gg (1); gametes G, g, G and g correctly derived (1); children's genotypes GG, Gg, Gg, gg correctly derived (1); gg clearly shown as having glycogen storage disease (1)
  d i XY
    ii XX (2)
  e Any three of: female will have two alleles; high chance that one is dominant (or described); male only has one X chromosome/one allele; so if recessive will have the disease (3)

2 a

0 marks	Level 1 (1–2 marks)	Level 2 (3–4 marks)	Level 3 (5–6 marks)
No relevant content	There is a basic description of two of: introduction of the gene from the bacterium to the corn DNA structure in relation to function assembly of amino acids into the protein	There is a clear description, but a lack of detail, of: introduction of the gene from the bacterium into the corn DNA structure in relation to function assembly of amino acids into the protein	There is a clear and detailed scientific description of: introduction of the gene from the bacterium into the corn DNA structure in relation to function assembly of amino acids into the protein

Examples of student answers:
The gene for the bacterial protein is introduced into the corn
This gene is a section of a DNA molecule
Enzymes are used to cut out the gene/section of DNA *or* There is a description of a possible method of how the gene is transferred, e.g. use a plasmid or virus
This DNA section has a specified sequence of bases which act as code for assembly of amino acids in the correct order to produce protein

  b Advantages [for full marks at least one advantage and disadvantage and a reasoned conclusion]: higher yield; less use of pesticides; only targets the corn borer
Disadvantages: possible effect on other organisms; concerns about human health; may increase numbers of other pests (3)
Reasoned conclusion (1)
3 a i Shape or colour/named example (1)
    ii Migration (1) (other acceptable, e.g. courtship behaviour)
  b i large surface area to volume ratio (1) to absorb soluble food materials (1)
    ii Protects tapeworm from enzymes (1) which would digest the tapeworm's body
    iii Holds tapeworm to the gut wall (1) prevents it being moved out of gut (1)
  c Full 6 marks awarded only if all three given terms are used in correct context; maximum 4 marks if only two terms used; maximum 2 marks if only one term described in context.
    • The sporozoites travel in the blood to the liver.
    • Sporozoites enter the liver cells.
    • In the liver, some of the sporozoites divide.
    • (Sporozoites) become merozoites.
    • Merozoites are released from the liver into the blood, where they enter the red blood cells.
    • (Some) merozoites turn into schizonts.
    • Schizonts burst the red blood cells releasing more merozoites.
    • This release coincides with the fever attacks.

13 Environmental change and the distribution of organisms

▶ 13.1

1 Very few plants grow there – those that do are very small, so there is little food for herbivores. Few herbivores results in few carnivores.
2 They eat prey so there will be less prey for other carnivores. The numbers of all predators could go down.

▶ 13.2

1 A square frame which may also be divided into a grid.
2 A line drawn between two points to make ecological measurements, e.g. between the top of a beach and the sea.

▶ 13.3

1 The experiment is repeated by the same person with the same apparatus and the results are the same.
2 The method of the investigation must be suitable to answer the question being asked. Only the independent variable should affect the results, all other variables must be controlled.

▶ 13.4

1 Any three of: temperature, rainfall, light, oxygen levels, carbon dioxide levels, pH, pollution levels, e.g. sulfur dioxide.
2 a Lichens
  b Invertebrate animals
3 There should be more varieties of lichen and there should be greater numbers of each type.

▶ 13.5

1 Climate change has caused it to become warm enough further north for the birds to nest, and possibly too warm further south.
2 Any one of: use of chemical sprays by farmers, viral disease, changes in flowering patterns due to climate change.

Answers to end of Chapter 13 questions

1 Any three of: water, light, temperature, oxygen levels.
2 The birds will lose nesting sites, shelter and may lose a food source.
3 A line is marked between two points and then the quadrat is placed at regular intervals along the line. The organisms in the quadrat are counted.
4 The mean is the total of all the readings divided by the number of readings. The median is the middle value of the readings when written in order.
5 A measurement is reproducible if the investigation is repeated by another person, or by using different equipment or techniques, and the same results are obtained.
6 There are so many variables which are difficult to control.
7 A data logger – a computer attached to sensors.
8 The results measure the long-term effects of changes in the atmosphere and the scientist does not need to leave expensive equipment out in the investigation area.

9 Advantages: the data logger takes readings at regular intervals, does not depend on different people (human error) to read temperature, can be calibrated to take accurate readings. Disadvantages: expensive equipment, requires a power source and access to computers.

10 There are so many possible variables. It may be obvious that the climate has got warmer but this may lead to other changes. For example, if a plant flowers earlier in the year, the insects which feed on it may not be around to pollinate the flowers. This could lead to a fall in the number of plants and also in the number of insects which would normally feed on the nectar.

14 Human population and pollution

14.1
1 Land has to be cleared, which destroys their habitats.

14.2
1 The oxygen content of the water decreases until there is little oxygen left.

14.3
1 Sulfur dioxide
2 Damage to trees means birds lose food and habitats.

14.4
1 Photosynthesis
2 Respiration during decay by microorganisms

14.5
1 Carbon dioxide is removed from the air by plants in photosynthesis and by dissolving in oceans, rivers and lakes.
2 If the climate gets warmer, the ice will melt.

14.6
1 The climate has changed anyway, even before humans evolved.
2 Between 1880 and 1910, the temperature decreased by about 0.5 °C. After 1910, the temperature gradually rose but dropped during several years until the 1980s when it continued to rise until 2000 when it seems to level off.

Answers to end of Chapter 14 questions

1 Chemicals used to kill weeds
2 Nitrogen oxides
3 The clouds of gas are blown by the wind.
4 Methane is produced by cattle and from rice growing.
5 Burning the felled trees releases carbon dioxide. When the trees decay, carbon dioxide is released due to respiration of microorganisms.
6 Any three of: herbicides, pesticides, fertiliser, toxic chemicals from landfill, untreated sewage.
7 There is a loss of habitat for all the animals which live in trees, e.g. birds and insects and less food for some organisms.
8 If we take peat from the bogs, the microorganisms in the garden soil decay the peat. This releases carbon dioxide into the atmosphere and the carbon which had been 'locked up' in the peat is no longer sequestered. The increased carbon dioxide can contribute to global warming.
9 High levels of mineral ions, such as nitrates, stimulate the rapid growth of algae and other water plants.
Competition for light increases and many plants die.
Microorganisms feed on the dead plants.
Respiration by the microorganisms depletes the oxygen concentration in the water.
Most of the aerobic organisms die due to lack of oxygen.
10 Human activities cause an increase in greenhouse gases. Energy is radiated back to Earth from the greenhouse gases in the atmosphere and warms the planet.

15 Evolution

15.1
1 Characteristics which we develop during our lifetime, e.g. developed muscles, hair colour due to dyeing it.
2 Charles Darwin

15.2
1 Natural selection
2 Finches on the Galapagos Islands

15.3
1 Variation is due to differences in their genes.
2 They had a mutated gene, which gave them immunity to the disease.

15.4
1 Animals, plants, microorganisms
2 They show the relationships between organisms.

15.5
1 Any one of: bones, teeth, shells, claws.
2 The fossils have been destroyed by Earth movements or other climatic conditions, or the fossils were not formed in the first place because the conditions were not suitable.

15.6
1 It eats all the animals of that species.
2 Volcano, earthquake, tsunami, collision by asteroid

15.7
1 It may be too hot or too cold for the organism to survive, the food supply might change.
2 A new disease being introduced into the population. It is unlikely to be a new predator because dinosaurs were at the top of the food chain.

15.8
1 Islands break away from the mainland, new rivers form, mountain ranges or craters separate them.
2 The wide range of alleles that control the characteristics in a population

Answers to end of Chapter 15 questions

1 a About 4.5 billion years
  b About 3.5 billion years ago
2 Early life forms were soft-bodied and did not form fossils.
3 3×10^9
4 The original species may be left with too little to eat.
5 A giant asteroid colliding with Earth; due to sea ice melting and cooling the sea temperature by about 9 °C.
6 Any three of: the climate may change – it could become hotter, colder, wetter or drier; a new predator may move into the area; a new disease may affect the population; a new competitor for the food supply may move into the area; there may be a loss of habitat such as nesting sites.
7 Lamarck suggested that characteristics which developed during the lifetime of the organism could be passed on. Darwin said that organisms with the best characteristics survived to breed and the offspring inherited the characteristic.
8 If the offspring are produced by sexual reproduction, then the genes of both parents are inherited in different combinations when the gametes fuse.
9 Those that are best adapted or suited to their environment live long enough to breed. The weaker ones may die before they breed.
10 Evolutionary trees show the relationships between organisms and whether they had common ancestors.
11 Two populations of an organism become separated and live in two different regions, e.g. two sides of a new river, either side of a mountain range.
12 Reference to isolation of two groups; there is genetic variation in the two populations; alleles are selected which give an advantage; interbreeding no longer possible (as populations diverge/become different); therefore new species are formed (speciation).

16 Energy and biomass in food chains and natural cycles

16.1
1 Plants capture light energy and transfer it to chemical energy. They make food which is then eaten by animals. Plants start the process of energy transfer in living organisms.
2 Sunlight

16.2
1 Respiration
2 Insert a temperature probe (attached to a data logger) inside a vacuum flask containing the peas.

16.3
1 To prevent them using (wasting) energy for movement, and to maintain their body temperature. The energy is used for growing (meat production).
2 How far food must be carried from the farm to the shop or table.

16.4

1 The population could become extinct if the young fish don't grow and reproduce.
2 The fungus *Fusarium*

16.5

1 Worms
2 Microorganisms (bacteria and fungi) which breakdown/digest waste materials from animals and plants or dead organisms.
3 This depends on the method chosen, e.g. rate of carbon dioxide production could be measured, qualitative observations can be made to judge how quickly the material is decaying (becoming more mouldy).

16.6

1 Photosynthesis
2 Something which 'locks up' more carbon than it releases.

Answers to end of Chapter 16 questions

1 The mass of living material
2 Compounds containing carbon/carbon dioxide. One of carbohydrate/fat/protein/named example of one of these.
3 Respiration and combustion (burning)
4 Reduce the number of stages. Carnivores have less energy available than herbivores who only eat plants. Rear animals indoors.
5 They start the process of decay by eating dead animals or plants and produce waste materials. Decay organisms then break down the waste.
6 Green plants or algae
7 The microorganisms decay the garden waste. The energy from respiration heats up the surroundings.
8 There are fewer stages in the food chain so less energy is wasted by eating herbivores than carnivores.
9 The processes that remove materials from the environment are balanced by processes that return these materials.
10 There is undigested food in the faeces (cow dung), urea is lost in the urine, the calf transfers energy to move around, the calf produces methane which is lost to the atmosphere, the energy released in respiration is eventually wasted heating the surroundings.

Answers to examination-style questions

1 a i Cube A = 3:1 (2) 24:8 or wrong answer but correct calculation (1)
      Cube B = 1.5:1 (2) 96:64 or wrong answer but correct calculation (1)
   ii Long and flat or other suitable description (1)
  b (Because smaller organisms have a larger surface area to volume ratio) they will lose heat faster (1) maintaining a suitable temperature for enzymes/metabolic reactions (1)
  c Oxygen is required for respiration (1) energy from respiration is required for growth (1)
  d Any four of: mature organisms are larger (1) larger organisms overheat (1) fewer survive/mature (1) to reproduce (1) so the population will decrease (1) *or* mature organisms are larger (1) smallest mature organisms will survive (1) they will reproduce (1) the numbers of smaller fish will increase (1)

2 a Any two of: same volume of solution [do not allow 'same size of container'; left for same length of time; same temperature; same oxygen; same pH; same number of invertebrates/animals [do not allow 'same number of species']; same age/stage of invertebrates/animals (2)
  b Line of best fit/curve/point to point drawn going through 240–260 and 25 (1), correct interpolation to *x*-axis (1) [if no work on graph, allow 250]
  c i (C) 50% killed at lowest/low copper concentration (1) [ignore 'least survivors']
   ii Any two of: involves counting; easy to do invertebrates as more sensitive; needs less/no apparatus (2)